*This book is dedicated to my wife, Christine, the love of my life, and our two boys, Mathias and Sheldon, who make our life interesting and full. Most importantly, I want to thank my Lord and Saviour, Jesus Christ, for changing my life completely.*

# THE Harpist
### EDUARD KLASSEN

## A SOULFUL JOURNEY

### THE UNTOLD STORY

Printed in Canada

Photo Credits:
Menno Colony Archives
Eduard & Christine Klassen
Mary Layton
Gus Sarino

Book Design, Cover & Layout:
Gabriela Altman

Writer and Editor: Lois Neely
*We thank you Lois for your patience, as you worked with inexperienced people when it comes to writing stories. It was a pleasure to work with you, and thank you for your dedication until this book finally came to fruition, after 2 long years.*

For more information,
CD and DVD orders or concert bookings,
write to:
Eduard & Christine Klassen
CIM Inc.
P.O. Box 541, Stratford, Ontario N5A 6T7

Phone: (519) 271-2064
Toll Free: 1-888-855-5537
Fax: (519) 271-5070

E-mail: harp@eduardklassen.com

Visit our website at: www.eduardklassen.com

*table of contents*

Preface  .

Preface:

*As you read this little book,*
          *as you listen to the music,*
*I pray that you will hear not only a beautiful melody*
          *or entertaining words,*
*but you will also hear a message*
*of God's love*
          *and joy*
                    *and peace —*
*because of God's amazing, saving grace.*

*The grace that reached out to a little boy*
          *deep in the South American jungle,*
*that saved him and brought him*
*to play music for the Lord*
          *on stages all over the world.*

*TO GOD BE ALL THE GLORY AND PRAISE!*

Eduard Klassen

*Road through village in the Chaco*

*Bottle Tree in the Chaco*

*Nature in the Chaco*

# PART ONE –

# JUNGLE LIFE

Co-op in Paratodo

Native Woman

This house is where I was born

# my carefree childhood

We were happy, my Mom and Dad and five brothers. I remember waking up every morning to bird songs in the jungle just outside our mud house. The sun seemed to shine every happy, warm day so we didn't have to wear a lot of clothes — just shorts and bare feet.

*Cactus in the Chaco*

We spent all our life outdoors. As soon as my mother fed us breakfast of dried bread with wild honey, and milk from our own cows, we'd dash off to play in our beautiful, green jungle world. The Spaniards called it "The green hell" but it was the only world my brothers and I knew and we loved it.

We didn't know we were deep in the heart of South America, well south of the equator in a little country called Paraguay which is about twice the size of Great Britain but with scarcely 1/14th of the population. We didn't know we lived 120 kilometres (75 miles) from the Mennonite colony's main center. We only knew that sometimes our Dad with some of the other men in our colony would hitch horses to big farm wagons loaded with peanuts and cotton they'd grown, and head to the big town to sell their crops and also to buy things like sugar, flour and cooking oil. They had to travel a rough track through the bush. Usually the river beds were dry, but in rainy season the roads would be muddy so they would be gone for a week or two, but to little boys it seemed forever.

Our grandparents lived close-by in their own grass-roofed mud house. They had a little farm with cows and chickens. We liked to gather the eggs, those chickens had so many hiding spots it was a game to see who could find them first. Sometimes we helped hoe and weed their garden. We liked best going into the bush with grandfather to look for the cows that had wandered off, to make sure they were OK.

We had lots of delicious wild cactus berries, and we shinnied up the palm trees and with machetes hacked off the *palmas* fruit. Our people planted bananas, oranges, lemons, guava and grapefruit so we had lots of fruit to feast on.

My father was very good at gathering wild honey. We couldn't go with him because the bees got very angry when he stole their hives. Sometimes, though, we watched from a distance as he tiptoed towards the hive with a smoking rag "to put the bees to sleep," then when they stopped buzzing, with a big stick he knocked the hive to the ground and ran away fast. Later they built beehives like we have in Canada.

My parents also had a little farm, with a garden, five cows, some chickens and pigs. I was proud when my Dad let me help him build fences for corrals for the cattle, and soon I was helping clear the bush with a small axe and spade so he could grow more feed for the cows.

Every house had their own little "out-house" or latrine – just a wood shanty at the end of the garden, with a bench inside with one hole over a deep pit. Our mother put the ashes from the wood fire down that hole "to keep it sweet" she explained. Sometimes those horrible big frogs got down there, and big rats too. And there were other creepy bugs, and spiders that spun big webs in the corners. I did not like that shanty. We boys would not go into that out-house after dark, it was too scary.

*Paraguayan Toilet*

The little village we lived in had one dirt track running down the middle with seven or eight mud houses on each side. That's the way the Mennonite farmers lived. They each had carved their own farm lands out of the jungle for raising crops, but they put their houses close together for protection against any hostile savage Indians. Not all the Indians were as friendly and helpful as the ones who lived near us, some of them worked for my father when he started a brick factory. By the time I was born (1960) there were about 60 villages just like ours scattered throughout this remote jungle wilderness area.

One of the biggest problems in the colony was getting good drinking water. My father had dug a well but some big snakes had fallen into it and couldn't get out — it was about five metres (16 feet) deep. If those nasty snakes died they would poison our well for sure. And there were frogs down there. Have you ever seen a Paraguayan frog? Those crazy things are so big, the size of a small cat — I hated them and was careful not to step on them. They were sitting all around the moist edge of the well and some had fallen in. "We've got to get them out," my father said, "but first we'll have to kill them. Bring me a sling-shot!" he told me.

I raced to get it. Wow! - this was exciting. I was just a little kid, we had no television, no entertainment of any kind, so my brothers and I were eagerly waiting to see how my dad would shoot these snakes and frogs. "Stay back from the edge, boys," he warned us. It was very dangerous because that slippery dirt went all the way to the top, and if you weren't careful you could easily slide into the well. There was about a metre and a half (five feet) of water at the bottom.

But I was so excited to see Dad kill those big snakes that I came up close to watch. Oh! oh! — Just as he had warned, the dirt gave way and I slid head first into that deep well with that big bunch of snakes and frogs. It was horrible. I could swim so I wasn't afraid of drowning — but those snakes were around me and those crazy big frogs.

*Rattlesnake*

I screamed my lungs out: "Dad, get me out of here! The frogs and snakes are all around my neck!" My Dad threw a rope, I grabbed it and my strong big Dad pulled his oldest son out of that well. I will never forget it. Next time when Dad warned: "Don't come too close," I stayed away. I have never fallen into a well since!

My brothers and I had other friends to play with, kids who were part of our little colony of Old Colony Mennonites who spoke High and Low German. We didn't know how strange that was, for us little kids to be chattering away in a very old European language, in a new land where Spanish and the Indian *Guarani* are the official languages. And as well, we learned to speak the language of the Indians who lived among us and were our friends.

One of the favorite things we did was go hunting in the bush. As brothers we enjoyed ourselves doing all kinds of things – building little mud houses and making nice roads through the jungle, climbing trees, falling down from trees – we had lots of fun. We never dreamt that we were poor people, we thought we were the richest guys in the world. There is nothing to complain about my background,

I had an absolutely amazing time. I will never forget those beautiful nights and beautiful days of my childhood.

One day when my brothers and I were deep in the Paraguayan bush enjoying ourselves, the loudest thunder we'd ever heard came rolling over the bush and we thought it was a big storm coming. But we looked up through the branches and couldn't see any clouds. Then we saw a little dot with this beautiful white tail moving across the blue sky. It was the most amazing sight we had seen in our young lives. We didn't know what to think. I remember my brothers and I dropped everything and raced home. "Mom and Dad, did you see what we saw? Did you hear that loud thunder?" we yelled. Yes, they had heard the thunder and seen the dot and long white tail. "What was it?" we asked.

*Road through Chaco bush*

"We have an idea, but we're not sure. We think that little dot was an airplane, filled with people flying from one country to another," Mom and Dad told us.

I looked at my parents dumbstruck: "The one we saw had no people in it," I insisted. I couldn't figure out how people could fit into a tiny dot like that. It was just so small. For us it was amazing that we had seen a thing flying through the sky with many people in it.

Many, many times after that we saw planes flying. Many times my little brothers and I were sitting there watching up in the sky, watching the long white tails drifting by, with this loud thunder rolling over. In about 10 minutes, it was gone. Many times we were wondering, will we ever see something like that up close? Are those people different than we are? How can they fly and we can't? — I never dreamed that one day I would have the privilege to sit in a plane like that, flying from one country to another.

– ◆◆◆ –

# the long Mennonite journey

We wondered a lot about the world beyond our green jungle home. We had seen a few cars and a tractor or two. But a plane? Or a boat for people to ride in? – that was beyond us. "Tell us about the big boat you came on to get to this place," we used to beg our grandparents. And they would tell us about the tall ocean liner with many rooms and lots of people, sailing on a wide, wide ocean with no land in sight — we couldn't imagine what they were talking about. They told us about the long ocean voyage from cold, cold Canada to this very hot (120 F/49°C) primitive jungle home.

"But why did you pack up all your things and come here?" we would ask. They had told us what a wonderful country Canada was, how fertile the fields were, and the big crops they could grow on the rolling Manitoba prairies, the fat cows giving rich milk and healthy chickens dropping perfect brown eggs. So why did they leave?

"It's a very long story, are you sure you want to hear it?" Grandfather would say, settling back in the rocking chair he had made from wood in the bush, lighting up his own rolled cigarette. "Yes! Yes!" we'd shout.

*A typical farmhouse that was left behind in Canada*

And then he would tell us about a man called Menno Simon who was born many years ago, in 1496, in a land far away called Europe. He was a priest in the Roman Catholic Church who read his Bible, and like Martin Luther, decided to leave the church for a simple salvation by faith alone, and a simple, peaceful lifestyle. Many people, especially in South Germany and Switzerland, followed this new teaching even though it made the formal church leaders very angry. So angry that they brutally persecuted the followers of Menno.

"In the Netherlands, our home country," Grandfather would tell us, "during the middle 1500's, some 2000 Mennonites were killed for their faith. Many chose to leave Holland, some fled to the new colonies in America.

*A*SOULFUL JOURNEY

Our ancestors along with many others escaped to Germany where they were welcomed, probably because many people there had followed the German priest Martin Luther when he too left the Roman Catholic Church so they were sympathetic to other dissidents.

"But in Germany our people grew to be so many that there was not enough land left, where would young people settle?  Just about then, neighboring Russia was looking for farmers to settle a district they called '*The Ukraine*'.  They promised the Mennonites good land, with freedom of religion and language, and freedom from taxes and military service.  So in 1789 the first Mennonites moved from Germany to Czarist Russia.

*Saying Goodbye in Canada 1926*

"Again our people prospered — Mennonites work hard, they help each other and make good farms," Grandfather reminded.  "But over the next 100 years politics changed dramatically, and our people began to be persecuted.  They were forced into military service, they lost the right to their own language or to own property.  Thousands moved to America.

"Our ancestors were among the first group of German-speaking Mennonites to come from Russia to Canada, in

*My Grandparents came with this ship from Canada*

1874, to a broad fertile land much like what they had left in the Ukraine, in southern Manitoba hugging the American border.  Again they prospered, living peacefully among their neighbors, speaking their own Low German language, practicing pacifism and faith in God.

"But again trouble came to them," Grandfather continued.  "After the first Great War, anti-German feeling began to spread through Canada, and our faith and way of life was threatened.  No longer would Canada guarantee freedom

*Moving into the Chaco Wilderness by Oxen and Wagons.*   for our own German schools.

"We heard that the far away country of Paraguay was offering cheap land to Mennonites, with the right to our own churches and German language schools, and with exemption from military service.

"My father, your great-grandfather, in 1927 sold our farm, packed up our belongings and moved away from modern civilization. We headed south, hoping that finally we would find a place where we could be safe and live in peace. We were part of the first 279 Low German-speaking Mennonite families who would settle in Paraguay, in an area where no white people had ever lived.

"We were many weeks on the big ocean traveling from the frozen north to the hot tropical south. It was not easy. When we arrived, we found that our Promised Land was not yet surveyed so we were crowded into a makeshift settlement in a place called *Puerto Casado*. It was so tough that many people wanted to move straight back to Canada, but they had no money so they were stuck.

"We were stranded there for almost a year. The water was not good and 168 of our people died from typhoid fever, including one of your great grammas. Your other great grandmother was also very sick but God had mercy on her and healed her and made her the midwife of our colony, she brought more than 500 babies into the world! And she lived in Paraguay until she was 103!

"At last we made our way to our Promised Land, walking and by ox-cart, over mud tracks, 145 kilometres (90 miles) through bush and jungle, driving the beef and dairy cattle we'd been able to buy plus oxen and donkeys. We also took pigs and chickens with us into the jungle. Along the way we ate dried meat and Paraguayan dried bread – '*galletas*'," Grandfather told us.

*Natives Working*

Finally my great-grandparents got to their land, a big region called "*The Chaco*". Part of the area was grass-land, or "*Campos*," so they settled there first and plant-ed their first crops. There were no roads, no electricity, no running water. To build houses they had to make bricks with mud, and cut grass for the roofs. They had to dig wells and latrines. Later they learned that the soil in the jungle was more fertile than the grasslands so they beganclearing little plantations in the bush.

The cattle wandered through the bush and grew fat.

*Settling in the Chaco*

*A* SOULFUL JOURNEY

But first those early settlers had to make peace with the seven savage aboriginal tribes who had lived there forever.  The *Lengua* Indians from the beginning were helpful and became our friends and lived among us, we learned their culture and language.  But the other six tribes resented the white men intruding.  One tribe, the *Moros*, attacked and killed several Mennonites before a truce was called.  When the others saw how the Mennonite colonies were prospering, many decided to move near us so they could work for us.

# my first home

When I was born in 1960 our little colony by then was over 30 years old, and had grown to many little villages with other more modern Mennonites coming from Europe.  Life had been hard for these pioneers. Those farmers from Manitoba had no idea what they were running into. They had never experienced temperatures of 49°C! (120 F) When they planted the first wheat

*Building a Roof with Grass*

it all died.  Their first crops of peanuts and cotton failed because of draught, or the grasshoppers came and ate everything.  It was a very poor life, but still they were living their own peaceful, German Mennonite life-style without persecution, in that beautiful Paraguayan jungle – well, except for the savage Indians.
We kids never got over our fear that they might be lurking around the next big tree.

My parents were both born in Paraguay during the 1930s.
It was the expectation among Mennonites that young people had to work and help their family until age 21 before they could marry.
Once married, my Mom and Dad had to clear some land for themselves, get a garden growing, and build their own two-room mud-brick house with mud floor and grass roof.

*A replica of our first house in the Chaco*

To make the mud bricks they'd get a 200-gallon barrel and in it mix mud, grass and cow manure. They'd dump this smelly mess into wooden forms shaped like bricks and put them in the sun to dry and harden. Then they'd build the house walls with these mud bricks, and smear them with cow dung – that was the kids' job.  It made the walls hard and shiny, and kept the rain out.  Mother smeared the mud floors with a mixture of old eggs and milk to give them a shiny, hard finish.
–Whew! – it smelled horrible.

That's where I was born, in a little mud-brick house, the first of six boys.
We slept on mats mother made by stuffing flour sacks with dried grasses.
The cockroaches and blood-suckers loved those mattresses, they'd come out

*A*SOULFUL JOURNEY

at night and bite us and we'd wake up with blood all over — it was awful. Whatever clothes we had, my mother sewed by hand out of flour sacks. My Dad was a blacksmith and also made buggies.

– ◆◆◆ –

# school days plus siesta pranks

When I was five years old, my parents decided I should go to school. They were so proud that they were able to send their oldest son. I remember dressing for that first day in a new shirt. I walked two kilometers barefoot each way. I remember being in that beautiful classroom – it was just a mud-brick two-room building, but I was with my friends. I had never thought God would do such a wonderful thing in my life.

Conditions were very poor but many things were sent to us from Germany, Canada, and the States, such as books and blackboards for the teacher to write on. But I had no idea what he was writing. We had no paper for the first couple of years, we scratched our work on a piece of slate. Then I had to spit on it and wipe it with a rag so I could write on it again – that wasn't very sanitary. Once in a while we got some paper, and we had a primitive pen – just a piece of wood with a metal point stuck on the end, a nib I think they called it. We'd dip that nib into a bottle of iodine and write on the paper. It was such a mess that most of the time we just used the slate to write on. In the books people sent to us I saw pictures of far away places, and wondered if I would ever see anything like that. I never dreamed that God had such wonderful things in store for me.

*Older 3 brothers, Eduard, Wilfried, Viktor*

Unfortunately, our teacher, many times during the day would leave the class and sit for what seemed like hours in the outhouse smoking cigarettes. We had to sit still and weren't allowed to talk to our friends.I tell you, there was discipline in that school. Once, I was put over a chair and spanked with a rubber belt on my backside in front of the whole class. My brother just younger than me got many spankings.

Our family was very poor, among the poorest in the colony. The other Mennonites made us feel as if they were better than we were because they were richer, and that was hard to take. "You are just the Klassen boys, you are poor!" they'd taunt us. One day that really got to me. I was walking

*A SOULFUL JOURNEY*

home from school, and there was a strict way we had to do it or we were in big trouble with parents and teachers. We had to walk in order and very straight down the roads, and we had to salute or say "Hi " to older people.

I remember one day my friend Rudy and I were walking home from school. I thought he was my best friend, but that day he was bugging me, pinching me and making fun of me. I was getting very frustrated with him and finally I'd had enough and I turned around and punched him in the head with my fist. I didn't know he had a sore on his ear and when I punched him the blood came pouring out. Just then I heard the cling, cling of a bicycle bell behind me, and guess who was there? Our teacher! We didn't know he'd been pedaling his bike very slowly behind us and he'd witnessed the whole episode.

He didn't say a word, just sailed past us and went straight to Rudy's parents and then to mine. He told them his version of the story. When I got home I got a spanking from my Dad with the rubber strap on my backside. And the next morning in school, in front of 30 students the teacher gave me another spanking with a rubber fan belt. That really hurt, not physically as much as emotionally, I was angry and humiliated. The only thing that eased the pain was that Rudy got the same punishment.

We all have to learn from our mistakes. But sometimes it was hard. During those years I remember sometimes not having any food to eat. I hadn't had much for breakfast and I didn't have any food for lunch. I was so hungry I begged other kids for food. Although I lived with my family those years in absolute poverty, I thank the Lord that we didn't know we were poor. Today I live in such a beautiful place, how will I ever be able to thank Jesus for the changes He has made in my life! Because of that earlier poverty, I can be more thankful for what I have now, and I never want to take for granted that God has blessed me with so much.

# siesta time

We always had siesta time in Paraguay. In that part of the country it got very hot, up to 49°C (120 F). A normal summer day would be between 35°- 48°C (95 -118 F). So Mom and Dad, like all the other grownups would take a nap in the heat of the day for two or three hours. We boys could play quietly. We didn't have any toys, no little cars to drive around, but we always found something to make life a bit more interesting. Sometimes it was BIG mischief.

I remember one afternoon sitting on the eating table with my brothers in the kitchen waiting for our parents to get up. Our house had two rooms, the kitchen and the other room where Mom and Dad were sleeping. This day we decided to make sling-shots so we could hunt some birds. I needed to cut the rubber and the ropes but our knives were not sharp. I looked around for something that would do the job. I saw Dad's razor on the shelf, but we were not allowed to touch it because blades were very hard to get in the jungle. Mom and Dad were asleep, they'd never know, I figured. So I told my brothers: "Guys, get Dad's razor from the shelf, it's sharp, let's see how it works." So they hopped up and got the razor.

*Flower in Chaco*

Now this was an old fashioned style razor that you could hold in your hand, I had no idea how sharp it was. The table we were working on was brand new and I didn't want to cut on it in case I scratched it. So I said to my brother Wilfried: "Put the rope over your leg and I'll cut it." He put the rope across his leg, and I made a straight 10cm. (4-inch) cut straight through the rubber — and right through my brother's skin and all the way to the bone! When I saw that 4-inch cut coming wide open and the blood shooting straight at me – I'll never forget that picture. I screamed and so did Wilfried, so did the rest of the guys. Mom and Dad came running. I was covered with blood, so was Wilfried – everybody had blood on them. Mom and Dad didn't know who else was cut. Finally they understood that only Wilfried had the cut on his leg, no one else.

Since there were no hospitals, Mom and Dad tied up Wilfried's leg until the bleeding stopped. My poor brother was yelling like crazy, he cried for hours after that, and for days and nights to come, that poor guy. It's amazing that he didn't bleed to death, it was a miracle.  We didn't even stitch it up, there was no one who could do that.  When everything was calmed  down my Dad asked: "Eduard, how did this happen?"  I was scared that if I told him the truth, I'd get a spanking. So I said I'd found an old razor out in the yard .

My Dad went to check the shelf where he kept his razor and saw that one brand new blade was missing. Oh boy, I was in trouble. Not only had I done something very bad to my brother, which was an accident in a way, but I had lied about it. "And for this you are in big trouble," my Dad said. And he gave me one more won-derful lesson which helped me not to lie in the future.  But you know, spankings are sometimes not enough, each person has to make a personal commitment to do the right thing.  I learned from very young that lying doesn't get you far, it only gets you into big trouble.

– ◆ –

Lots of things happened in my childhood years during siesta time when my parents were sleeping. I confess we boys were not always obedient during siestas – this was the time for fun. I remember one very hot day we begged our parents to let us go swimming in the water hole behind our house and they said absolutely no way. "Can we go hunting for birds with our sling-shots?" we begged. And as usual, they said O.K.  We were used to being in the bush, we knew how to watch out for the dangerous rattlesnakes which were in great abundance.

*Dugout in the Chaco*

But our idea wasn't to go hunting, we headed for our l0 x 20 metre (35′ x 65′ ) water hole about a kilometre (not quite a mile) away from home.  As soon as we were there, off with the pants and into the water. My, it felt so good, so refreshing. There is nothing better on a hot day than a water-hole to swim in.  We could all swim except our youngest brother who sat and watched us.

We made a big mud slide sloping down into that cool water. Wow, it was just incredible.There were bits of hard dirt and wood stuck in the mud, and needles from the *algarobo* trees. But we didn't care that it was rough and our butts were getting sore, we were having a great time sliding down, splashing into the water.

After about 20 trips down, our rear ends were all red and scratched and we decided we'd had enough of that – now was the time to teach our little brother how to swim. So we picked him up by the arms and legs, and started to swing him out over the water. He was scared and screaming. But we counted "One! Two! Three!" and dropped him into the water. He came up sputtering and thrashing around, he was having trouble getting air. And then he went under again. We were laughing, we thought: "My goodness, this little guy is having a tough time learning how to swim." He came up again and managed to grab some grass and pull himself out of the water. We were just laughing so much that he had actually learned how to swim – we didn't realize he'd almost drowned.

And we didn't know our mother had arrived in time to see the whole thing, to see her baby almost drown while his brothers were all sitting there in the nude laughing their heads off. Oh Oh! My mother broke off a green switch from the bush, and as soon as she made sure my little brother was alright, we bigger boys all got a spanking. And what a spanking – we'd already scratched our rear ends on all those needles and pieces of dirt and sticks in the mud, and then to get warmed with a green stick on top of that – Ouch! That really hurt. I never forgot it.

*Lagoon in the Chaco*

I learned another lesson that day – that we should listen to our parents and do exactly what they say and not do something else. We'd almost killed our brother by drowning him in the water – that was one of the reasons my parents didn't want us to go swimming when they were not there to watch us. That was very dangerous.

I thank God that He had His Holy Angels protecting us and especially our little brother so that nobody was killed. Our God is an Awesome God! I don't expect my little brother ever forgot that day either.

– ◆ –

As the oldest of six brothers, when my Mom and Dad were not at home I was responsible to take care of my little brothers. And that was not always fun. Sometimes we got quite upset with each other. I remember Mom and Dad going many times to church in the evening which was about three kilometres (two miles) away from our home. They usually went by horse and buggy, leaving their children at home. That was a common thing, everyone did it like that.

But those were very scary evenings for us kids. We were always scared about the wild Indians in the bush.  As little children we always thought they were right there although we were really in no danger, and we had neighbors right across the street, native people who were our friends and we spoke their language. Still, we were scared of the wild Indians in the jungle. And we heard the big cats — the cougars, and all sorts of wild animals crying in the bush, it was scary. We had no electricity so each night we made a big fire in front of our house to keep the snakes and the millions of mosquitoes away from us. And the wild animals…

I remember one night Mom and Dad had gone to church. We kids sat around the fire and ate some watermelon and the juice dripped from our chins onto our bare chests. That night I was bored. I had a little pretend watch with a little plastic band on it, and I decided I wanted to make a hole in that band. How could I do it?

Now, Mom had a needle box which she always told us we were not to touch. But I knew there were lots of needles and crochet hooks in there, and that's what I need-ed. Mom wouldn't see it, I figured, I was just going to use it for a couple of minutes and put it right back. — So why not?

I opened Mom's needle box, took out a crochet hook, put that little plastic band onto my finger and pushed the crochet hook through, I pushed as hard as I could. And in

*Cactus Flower*

just a second this crochet hook went right through the band and right through my flesh all the way to the bone. I tried to pull it out but it had this little hook on the end and wouldn't come. The more I pulled, the more it hurt, terri-bly. I yelled and screamed and soon all my little brothers were crying too, they thoughtthis was the end of their old-est brother. I didn't know what to do.

So we all trailed across the street to our neighbors, our native Indian friends. We were all sticky and dirty and howling our heads off.  They wanted to pull this needle out, they didn't understand the little hook on the end. So when they pulled hard, I screamed louder than ever. It took a lot of explaining to make them understand it was not an ordinary needle but a crochet hook. And somehow it was hooked behind a muscle. We didn't have a hospital, but by this time there was a nurse with a little clinic about a kilometre away and my kind Indian neighbor took us kids there.

I didn't want to go because I'd heard they put needles under your skin when you were sick and they really hurt. But this Indian woman insisted and dragged us over there, we were all crying.

When we got to the clinic, my brothers, still crying, had to sit on a little bench while I went inside. And sure enough, here comes this nurse with a big needle. I screamed, boy, did I scream like I'd never screamed before. Outside, my brothers started yelling and screaming too. When I stopped, they stopped. When I cried, they cried. Finally this nurse pricked my finger and soon it was frozen, I couldn't feel a thing. Then she took out the crochet hook and we went home.

When my Mom and Dad came home and heard the whole story we were a bunch of frightened boys, we were scared to death. That night we learned a lesson, that when Mom or Dad said "Don't touch!", then we'd better not touch. I still have the scar on my finger, it may never go away. But my brothers and I all learned a valuable lesson that night.

*Algarobo Tree*

# i hear music!

I was only seven years old when something happened that changed my life forever. My Dad came home from town with a shiny black box, he turned a little knob and we heard someone speaking in our own language. It was a radio! We could only get one station on it – HCJB, the VOICE of the ANDES. Imagine that! – Here we were deep in the Paraguayan jungle, with the whole family sitting under the stars listening to our own German language coming out of that little box.

*Sunrise in the Chaco*

And I heard music like I'd never heard before. In our churches we sang only Gregorian chants, with no harmony and no instruments. But the music coming out of that box was like — I couldn't think what it was like, because it was like nothing I'd ever heard. It wasn't just people singing these lovely melodies and harmonies, there were other sweet music sounds and I wondered what was making them. No matter, I was thrilled. A seed was put in my heart that night that never died. I began to long to make that sweet music that spoke to my soul as nothing had ever done.

*Mother, grandparents, Eduard, 2 years old*

I was fascinated with this little box, this radio. Night after night I lay behind the box looking into it, trying to see the people who must be inside, talking and making music. I asked my Dad hundreds of questions.
I couldn't understand that those people were sitting in a studio thousands of miles away, across the mountains in Quito, Ecuador. And I never dreamed as I lay there looking up at the stars and marveling at the sweet sounds coming out of that little box, I never dreamed that someday I would meet many of these people in the box, and have the privilege of playing and raising funds for this wonderful missionary radio ministry – *The World Radio Missionary Fellowship* – that brought music to my heart, and a clear gospel message into our jungle home.

– ◆ –

# grandparents and growing pains

For my brothers and me to visit grandparents was always a great adventure. It was wonderful just to walk through the jungle. I remember one beautiful hot summer day when I was just a little boy of seven or eight. My brother and I had been visiting with our grandparents and now it was time to walk home, about two kilometres, (a mile and a half).

*Grandma and Grandpa Klassen*

It hadn't rained in a long time but clouds were gathering in the sky. "Go straight home, fast," Grandfather warned us. "The rain is coming, it looks like a bad storm up there."

But my brothers and I thought we had lots of time, two kilometres wasn't that far. So we dawdled along through the jungle. About half way home we came to a neighbor who had just finished plowing and he came running to the road where we were strolling along. "Boys, there's a big storm coming, you'd better run home as fast as you can." We really didn't believe this guy, we couldn't have cared less. We just enjoyed being by ourselves, we just kept sauntering along.

*My mothers family and their home*

We hadn't gone far when a big black cloud sailed low over the trees – it was a huge storm breaking all around us, from zero winds to gale force bending the trees over, breaking off the branches. The dirt was like sandpaper flying around us, hurting our skin so much because we had nothing on but shorts. We crouched down holding onto trees, screaming and thinking we cannot take this for long.

And then, praise the Lord, the rain came down, the wind died, the dust settled. In about 15 minutes the storm was over. Broken branches were lying all around us on the ground. With the final roll of thunder, my brother and I got up from behind the trees and started for home, running as fast as we could. And what a mess we found: our little house was still standing but part of the roof was gone. Inside our house there was mud all over the mattresses and the clothes. The whole ceiling had come down.

23

It was a frightening sight. Mom and Dad were not home, they were at the neighbor's a couple of hundred metres away (220 yards). When they found us we were all crying. "We thought you were at Grandparents' house — why did you come home in the storm?" they asked. We tried to explain to Mom and Dad what had happened. It was a very scary experience that really touched our young hearts. We had to praise the Lord that He had kept us alive once again. We could have been killed by those big flying tree branches, but God protected us.

– ◆ –

One day my grandparents came to stay with us while our Mom and Dad were away, we always had a lot of fun when they came. Remember, we didn't have the toys and computers that kids today have, but we had a big jungle right in our backyard with lots of wood to build toys. I remember putting poles in the dirt and making phone lines like we'd seen in the big town of *Loma Plata*. We made corrals with wood, then with smaller pieces of wood we made cows to put in the corral. When the big rains came, all our hard work was washed away and then we had to start all over again. We were never bored. When my parents weren't around, sometimes we did things we shouldn't do, we never ran out of ideas.

As the oldest I was expected to keep an eye on the younger boys. This day they were out in the yard somewhere and I noticed it was very quiet and that meant trouble. So I went and checked on them. I found the two youngest boys had built a beautiful corral with sticks and ropes, it was about five inches (12 cm) high. But instead of putting some wooden pretend cows in there, my fifth brother, Ronald, had come up with a new idea – he'd caught a big Paraguayan frog – yes, one of those huge ugly things. It weighed about a kilogram (about two pounds!) and was as high as the corral so it easily could hop out. So Ronald found a big five-inch nail and a hammer, he put that frog in the middle of the corral and hammered the nail straight through the frog!

When I got there, he had just finished the job and the boys were so proud of themselves. "You know what Eduard? This crazy frog kept hopping out of the corral and we couldn't keep it in. So we just nailed it down." I saw that poor frog begging for its life – it couldn't move an inch, its legs were sticking out on both sides. It was absolutely horrible. I was sorry to see that frog suffering and ran to the house to get Grandpa. "Come and look what Ronald has done." Grandpa took one look and felt sorry for the frog too. He got a spade and killed the frog so it wouldn't suffer any more.

Then he took my brother and gave him a spanking. It was the first spanking he'd given a grandchild and Grandpa felt so sorry that he gave my brother 10 *guaranies*. That was a lot of money, about $10! For 10 *guaranies* my grandfather could give me a spanking anytime. Anyway, that story I will never forget. My brother and I learned that you should never, never torture any animals, they feel pain too. I learned that day that other people thought the same as I did. God made those animals just as He made you and me, and we have to take care of them in the right way.

– ◆ –

I had to stay a lot at my aunt and uncle's places because their children were very small so I, as the oldest grandson had to help out. And because my parents were very poor, it was sometimes hard to put food on the table, so I had to help make money for the family. I remember one particular time I was with my Uncle Willie who lived about 12 kilometres (7 miles) away from us. He also lived in a little mud brick house but he seemed to be a lot better off than my Mom and Dad. I worked for him plowing the fields. Believe me, it is hard work for a 10-year-boy to be walking behind four big horses, with that plow cutting up all sorts of stuff like snakes and frogs— I'll never forget it.

They had quite a few acres of cotton and sometimes I helped pick the cotton. One evening as the sun was about to go down behind the trees, my uncle asked me to take the horse and buggy and go get the native people who were working for him in the cotton fields which were four or five kilometres (two or three miles) away right through the jungle. Now that was a lot of fun. I liked buggies

*Harvesting Cotton*

because I liked to drive them fast and my uncle didn't seem to mind. So I stood up on that buggy and whipped those horses to go fast through the bush. Oh man, did I love it! Those horses could really run.

I came around the first curve, around the second curve, and that is where I saw someone standing in the middle of the road. It was one of the poor Spanish farmers who lived in the bush. The native people I was to pick up had already left the fields and were there beside the road. All I had to do was load them onto the buggy, turn around and go back. And that is what I did, they jumped on and I began to turn around. But this poor farmer came closer, yelling at me and waving a gun in the air.

*A* SOULFUL JOURNEY

"Get off that buggy or I'll kill you," he screamed and pointed his gun at me. I turned around and looked at this guy, was he kidding? Why would he want to shoot me? And then the native people shouted "Get going, this guy's drunk – he'll shoot us!" The natives were pulling themselves up into the box, I looked back again just in time to see him raise the shiny revolver and BANG! The first bullet went over my head between the horses. BANG! BANG! BANG! – he unloaded the whole round while we raced away. God must have had His holy angels around us because not one single bullet hit us, and he'd been

*Native Indians working on a new road*

shooting from no more than 10 metres (30') away! I was really shaken and it was a long time before I wanted to go again to that corner where the drunken Paraguayan had shot at us.

The native people who'd been with me asked my uncle to let them use his rifle to go shoot this guy. But my uncle said, "No way, this poor guy was drunk. We'll help him out when he's sober again." But when they came next day to that area, the drunk had gone off into the jungle.

I always had a good time with my uncle and aunt. They taught me a lot of things, they also taught me about Jesus. O yes, I went to church with my parents every Sunday but it was boring. We had to sit still and listen for about an hour and a half of reading. And then those dull, tuneless Gregorian chants that meant nothing to me. I praise the Lord for the weeks I was with my uncle and aunt because they told me about a Jesus who seemed very real to them and again a seed was planted in my young heart.

– ◆ –

*Industry in Loma Plata*

## My first job

My Mom and Dad moved many, many times. Because they didn't have much to lose, they tried many things to make our life better. When I was about 12-years-old, my parents decided to move us to the colony's capital, *Loma Plata*, about 120 kilometres (75mi.) away. It was the most modern town in the Paraguayan jungle with some 1200 people living there, they even had electricity. Mom and Dad thought there was so much more for us children to do, and also some factories where my father thought he could get work. We were still very poor, my father had not been able to make a living with farming.

Soon after we moved, my parents asked one of the cotton factory bosses to hire me, and also my 10-year-old brother. It was very hard, sometimes working 12 hours a day for me, a little less for my brother, filling the tanks with cotton until they were full. It was a dirty job. Often there were rotten eggs that the chickens had laid in the cotton before it was shipped off to the factory, we'd pick them out and toss them against the wall. And then there were those ugly frogs and all sorts of dirty things. It was very unhealthy with dust and cotton flying all around, I coughed constantly, day and night. Still we considered it a privilege to be able to work there and earn money to help our family. I enjoyed it very much.

*Transporting Cotton in 1964*

We learned some tricks to play on the farmers who came with their loaded wagons to the cotton factory. Often they would come late in the evening and have to wait all night to unload, they would have to watch that load of cotton — and us. We worked all night and had lots of fun teasing these guys. One farmer was very rude to us, he'd laugh and swear at us, sometimes he went after us with his horse whip, and he had a sling-shot he knew how to use really well. We told him we'd steal the lunch he'd brought with him, the oranges, grapefruits and so on. Finally he dozed off and we grabbed his lunch – we weren't hungry, we just wanted some fun.

The farmer woke up and ran after us and that is exactly what we wanted. We knew every corner of that 80 x 20 metre (270'x65') cotton building, but the farmer didn't. There were many rooms with many containers, some filled with cotton five metres (16') deep. The farmer thought we'd jumped into one of these containers so he jumped in after us, and sank up to his neck in cotton. – He didn't know we were hanging onto a cable up top, laughing our heads off. We scampered away while he had to wait a couple of hours until someone came by and rescued him. He was very nice to us after that.

These factories were dangerous places. One day my friend reached in to clean some saws while the machine was still running, which he was not supposed to do. Suddenly the saws grabbed his hands and pulled him in, and in seconds my friend went straight through and was cut into tiny pieces.

*A* Soulful Journey

The older boys working in the factory taught us to smoke, and how to hide it from our parents.  I was soon smoking like a chimney, it took me 18 years to kick that bad habit.

My brother and I tried to work overtime because we could keep that money for ourselves to spend on anything we liked, the rest went to our parents. One day I made a lot of overtime money, so I headed to the store to buy what I'd been dreaming about for years — my first factory-made shirt!  It was an amazing shirt, I still have a picture of it. It was a proud day when my parents saw that their oldest son could save and buy his own shirt!

With overtime pay I also was able to buy a used guitar. I was so excited. The native people taught me how to play it, and every spare moment I tried to make music with that guitar. I tried to remember the melodies I'd heard on *HCJB* radio and picked them out. Those were some of my happiest moments.

*My First Bought Shirt 1972*

– ◆ –

One day my Dad came home with a beautiful, beautiful motorbike. It was an old BMW, one of the after-war German bikes. What an amazing machine! It had a big engine – WOW! It was so loud, so big and so tall. And it was a lot faster than horses! My Dad showed me all the little things that machine could do, how the engine worked, how many buttons it had. My Mom and Dad wanted to give their children more than what they had when they were little and so here we had this motorbike. I wanted to drive it so badly but my Dad would barely let me touch it. He was so fussy about it that he cleaned that motorbike just about every day to make it nice and shiny.

My Mom and Dad went away for three days leaving the six boys at home alone – with the motorbike. But I'm sure my Dad knew his boys had it all planned how they would use that motorbike. So just before he left, he took the key out of the bike and took it with him.

Now what could we do? Six young boys put their brains together, there had to be a way for us to have some fun with that motorbike. I remembered that one of my friends had told me you don't need a key to get the motorbike to work, all you need is to push a needle through the wire.  So I got my Mom's needle box, the one we were not allowed to touch – that was my first dishonesty. I pushed a needle through the wires and believe it or not, that green light on the BMW was shining and we knew we were all ready for the ride.

I had never driven a motorbike, but I had watched my Dad. I stood on the bike and cranked it up – and when that loud motor started up my heart just about fell out of my body. I was nervous, I was shaking, but I was smiling because we had this bike running. I was so small I couldn't touch the ground when I sat on it. My five brothers were standing around waiting to see what would happen next. I managed to push down the clutch on the left side and shoved the BMW into first gear.
I heard the noise going up loud and the wheels spinning at the back. I yelled to my brothers, "I'm ready, push me!"

And they pushed me off the long bike rest it was standing on and I was on my way. I was driving a motorbike! I was heading  across our yard, straight for the street,

*Nature in the Chaco*

and through town. That bike was so huge I laid across the tank and I could still barely reach the handlebars. But I was flying through town. Surely all my friends were watching and wondering: "Who is the little guy on the big BMW with his hair flying straight back, flying for the trip of his life?"

I made it the two kilometres (l.5 mi.) to the end of the street and managed to turn around and head back. When I drove into the yard my brothers were all standing there waving and cheering. Their big brother was riding a motorbike!  WOW! It was awesome.

But suddenly I realized I didn't know how to stop. "Guys, grab both sides of the bike", I yelled. And they did just that, and slowed me to a stop. Very carefully we smoothed over all the tracks in the sand, figuring we could keep this escapade top secret. Because if Mom and Dad figured out I had taken out the motorbike, I would be in BIG trouble.

But when they came home, just about the whole town showed up telling Mom and Dad what their children had done when they were away. When the last neighbor had gone home, my Dad said, "Children, come over here, I want to have a big talk with you."  He was not very happy, neither was my Mom. "Children, did you use the motorbike on the weekend?"

To spare us a warming on our butts, I said "Dad, you must be kidding. Don't you remember, you took the keys along, we did not drive that motorbike." My Dad was very sad, he knew that all those neighbors could not be lying, his children had to be.

"For lying, and for using the motorbike without permission, we will go inside and have a long talk and a very good spanking!" Dad said. And that spanking I will never forget. When Mom and Dad told us not use something, we should leave it alone.  I thank God for my Mom and Dad for helping us so many times. That story of the BMW I can never forget, I got a wonderful lesson from that.

# we move again... *and again...*

When I was 13-years-old, my Mom and Dad moved to live at a native reserve. The Mennonites had started schools and a medical clinic, and my parents went there to help out. Native Indians lived all through the area beside the Mennonite villages because they found they could benefit from the Mennonites' hard work.

*Horse and Buggy*

My Dad started a brick factory and ran it for a couple of years and we had a great time living among the natives there. We just kind of lived the same style as they did: we spoke their language, we played soccer with them, we worked together with them. None of us had television or telephones or any of that kind of entertainment that people had in the modern world. But thank God, we didn't know it, we didn't feel deprived or poor in any way.

One day Dad asked me and my nine-year-old brother Viktor to deliver a buggy to our grandparents who lived about 30 kilometres (20 miles) away, then ride the horses home. Wow! This meant a straight run through the Paraguayan jungle with the buggy. It was amazing that our Dad would let two young kids do it, we'd never done it before. Mom and Dad gave us all sort of warnings, how we should drive and not drive. We promised heaven and earth that we'd obey all those instructions – it would have been better if they'd said nothing!

*Native Neighbours*

I remember leaving our home, my brother and I, standing in the box behind the horses (the buggy had no seat). I was standing there holding the reins just like Ben-Hur in the movies. We left home slowly, just going easy, until we were a couple of kilometres (1.5 mi.) into the bush. "Let's go for it!" I yelled to my brother. This might be the only trip we'd have by ourselves, flying through the Paraguayan jungle.

With huge smiles on our faces, we whipped those horses until the dust was flying 10 metres (30 feet) high in the air behind us, we were going as fast as

*A*SOULFUL JOURNEY

those horses could go. The branches were flying above our heads and two little boys were screaming and yelling for the fun of their life!

At that pace it didn't take long to get to our grandparents place. When we drove into their yard, they came running out: "What are you boys doing here?" We explained that Dad told us to bring the buggy and then ride the horses home.

"But what's wrong with the horses?" Grandfather asked. "They're soaking wet!" Oh oh, it was dry season and there was no water in the bush. I tried to lie to Grandfather but he knew we'd driven those poor horses almost to death. I was in big trouble. But it's easier to make peace with grandparents and soon we were enjoying a big meal around their table.

When the horses were rested, it was time to head for home. I didn't want to leave — the sun was just about to go down, and we didn't have a buggy to protect us, and we couldn't go fast this time. My brother climbed up behind me on one horse and he held the reins of the second horse as it trotted along behind us.

*Sunset in the Chaco*

We said goodbye to Grandma and Grandpa, but we were not smiling, in fact we were scared to death of the 30 kilometre (20 mile) ride through the dark. Soon the shadows came down from the big trees and then the black night. And we were hidden on the trail by ourselves, all alone in the deep Paraguayan jungle, wondering what might happen to us. Were wild Indians out there with their bows and spears waiting to kill us? Or wild animals?

Slowly the moon came up brightening the jungle. Higher and higher it came until the sky was bright, we could see the trees all around us and the road stretching like a white line ahead. This isn't so bad, we thought.

But about two hours into the trip, suddenly the horses stopped and sniffed around and we knew something was not right. And then I saw something jump from a tree, just a big dark shape dashing towards us. The horses reared up, turned, and began running as fast as they could, back the way we had come. My little brother started to slide off the horse. He grabbed my shirt as he fell and now was hanging onto that shirt for dear life. "Eduard, I'm falling, I'm falling, I can't hold on anymore!" he screamed as the horses raced through the jungle. I was terrified, I was holding tight to the horse's mane trying not to slide off myself — holding on for my life. I wasn't screaming, just holding, and I thought: "You'd better not let go of your brother, he'd be a meal for whatever is chasing us!" We didn't know what it was, but the horses were sure scared.

After a couple of kilometres the horses stopped. I pulled my brother up and just held him, we were both so scared we were shaking. So we prayed: "Lord, have mercy on us, we don't know what to do."

Finally I said to my brother, "We have to keep going towards home," I felt that strongly. So I turned the horses around and set out once more. But when we got to the spot where something had jumped out of the tree and chased us, the horses refused to go forward. So we had to go back to our grandparents' house for the night.

They were astonished when we woke them up. Back home my Mom and Dad were crying and praying the whole night for us, they didn't know if we were alive or dead, there was no telephone to let them know we were OK.

Next morning we started out in daylight on that same stretch of road. When we got to that spot again we could see big paw prints running along behind the horses' hoof prints. It must have been the biggest cougar in the jungle!

Two very frightened boys made it safely home. We told Mom and Dad what had happened. I thank God that He brought us through this, He didn't let us fall, He kept us alive. God had something in store for us and I praise Him from the bottom of my heart that I could learn to follow Him.

# The Klassen Boys ... Trouble!

It seems, as I look back, that the Klassen boys were always getting into trouble of some sort, and usually the oldest boy – that was me – was the ring leader. Like the day my brother Viktor and I were supposed to go and help my Dad clear the jungle so we could plant more crops. He had about 50 natives working with him in a part of the jungle many miles away. We thought this would be a lot of fun. It was a beautiful summer day when we set out walking, my brother and I loved the bush. The road through the jungle was quite good by Paraguay standards, but I said to Viktor: "Why don't we go straight through the bush instead of going all the way around by road, we have lots of time." So we left our house in the colony behind us and walked into the deep bush. It was beautiful. We had no watch to tell us the time, but all the time in the world, we thought. There were no paths to follow, we just made our own way.

"We'd better keep our eye straight on the sun so we'll know we're going in the right direction," I said. We had an idea of where we were headed but were not very sure.

*Nature in the Chaco*

I took along a rifle and bullets just to keep us safe. We were 12 and 15 years old at that time.

This part of the Paraguayan bush was semi-desert without a tangle of undergrowth, and very hot. As the day went on the sun became hotter and hotter. We didn't know if we should walk farther, or stop and rest a little bit. Somewhere deep in the bush I became scared, realizing I didn't have a clue where we were. There were no roads. There were no measurements. And the sun was directly overhead so I had no idea which way east or west was. I knew we needed to walk south-west to get to where our Dad was working.

"Viktor," I finally admitted, "I have no idea were we are, I have no idea what direction we're going." Worst of all, I realized we'd been going in circles: "I think I've seen that tree before, and the one around the corner, I've seen that one too." We were stuck, and both so scared we started to cry. "We'll never see our family again," we thought. And we started to pray.

The sun was beginning to go down so that had to be west, we knew — but we didn't want to believe it. We thought the sun was going down in the wrong direction! We were so hungry, I remember shooting a wild chicken. I had a lighter so we could cook the chicken, (we always carried a lighter with us in the bush). But we didn't have any water, and at 45°C (113 F) we were becoming dehydrated and were not thinking straight.

We started walking again, and to our surprise came to a fence! Which way now? "Walking left does not make any sense," I decided. "Let's walk to the right." And we did. And praise the Lord, *right* was the right direction. If we'd walked left, we would have walked straight into the wilderness where there was no water, absolutely no water anywhere, and we would have died. We may have made it through the night but in the next couple of days we would have died for sure.

But by walking to the right we soon came to an area where I had been before. And after many more hours of walking we heard natives yelling in the bush and we knew God had brought us in the right direction. We were going toward the place where my Dad was working. God brought us safely there. When we told Dad what we had done he was very, very sad because we could have died. Praise the Lord, He once again had shown us that God is in control and cares for us even when we do foolish things and make huge mistakes.

*Road in the Colony*

– ◆ –

As I said earlier, lots of things happened during siesta time because that was when our parents had an afternoon nap. As I became older and had to work harder, I wanted to have a nap in the afternoon as well. And I wanted my little brothers to be quiet. I remember one day I came home from work very tired and wanted to sleep so badly. I lay down on the bed and tried to sleep but it was noisy outside with all the chickens and animals.

I had just about fallen asleep when somewhere in the house or yard I heard an animal screaming, like a cat in big trouble! I didn't want to get up, so called out: "Is someone playing with a cat?" No answer. The screaming stopped and I fell back to sleep. Then I heard that crazy noise again, like a cat howling and screeching for its life. Again I called out: "Is someone playing with a cat?" Again no answer so I tried to fall asleep again. But a third time the animal screeched really loud and by then I was so angry I jumped out of bed and ran around the house looking for the whatever was making this racket. I couldn't find anything. Then I heard it again, but by now the sound was fainter, the animal sounded half dead.

I checked every room until I came to the little shower room attached to the house. And when I opened the door I could not believe what I saw. There was a limp, almost dead cat hanging on a rope tied around its neck. And sitting in the corner was my fourth brother Gustav, slowly pulling the rope up and down. — When he pulled up, the rope tightened around the cat's neck cutting off its breath so it was quiet, when he let it down the rope relaxed its hold and the cat screamed for its life. When I came into the room this poor cat was barely alive.

I was so upset I punched my little brother with my fist in the head, as hard as I could. I knocked him out, and he fell onto his back. "I've killed my brother!" I was sure. I fell on top of him, begging him to please forgive me. And after a few seconds my brother looked up at me, got up and said he was sorry. Then I said sorry, and we agreed that we would never hurt each other again. We hugged each other and straightened out the problem.

The point I want to make with this story is that we should always think before we do something. I should not have hit my brother so hard. He should have thought before he hurt that cat. And we must learn to forgive.

I thank God for my teenage years with my brothers. Even though I was the oldest and was in charge, maybe that was not the best situation, but I thank God for the experiences I had. Still today we love each other as brothers, although we've all made mistakes. I hope I learned from those mistakes. When you are spending time together as a family, please try to always think about it. We have to love and care for each other.

– ◆ –

# my first trip outside

By the time I was almost 15, I had lived in the town with electricity, but I hadn't seen any paved roads, or real sidewalks. One day, one of my parents' friends invited me to drive with him to the big capital city of Asuncion 500 kilometres (310 miles) away where our people went to sell produce and buy food and oil. I was so excited, I'd only dreamed about this. I bragged to my friends that I was going on a BIG trip, to the BIG city. What an adventure!

The truck was an old 1945 red Volvo but it was awesome to me. I sat in the open back of the truck with some other boys, among the chickens and old cheeses and other produce going to market. The palm trees were whizzing by. The dust was flying behind the truck. And the road was very rough, with one pot-hole after another, and one broken bridge after another. Sometime during that trip we got a big rain and the dirt road was covered in water so that we couldn't drive anywhere. We were stuck for many days. And that is when I turned 15 – among the millions of mosquitoes and thousands of snakes – but I was having a wonderful time!

*Transporting Cotton*

Finally the road dried and we headed again for the capital city. And for the first time in my life I saw a mountain! Our colony was totally flat, like the prairies our families had come from. But now I saw a big blue bump in front of my eyes. We left the palm trees and mud road behind and came slowly up that mountain. And from there we could see the big sugar cane fields on the hills close to the Paraguayan River. It was night when we came over the mountain ( it was only a big hill really). And I saw the biggest miracle of my life – down in the valley about 30 kilometres (20 miles) away was the capital city with all its glamorous lights twinkling. Wow! For a 15-year-old boy it was the most exciting moment of my life.

But there was a big river between us and that city. I'd never seen such a river, not like the little dried-up streams through the jungle. And no bridge across the wide river. Instead, we had to drive the truck onto a little car ferry.

*A*OULFUL JOURNEY

Again I'd never seen a boat, let alone had a ride on one. I was so scared that the ferry wouldn't make it, but it seemed to swim along as if there was nothing on it. Amazing! I couldn't take in so many new things. The crossing took about twenty minutes.

In Asuncion we drove to the place where I was supposed to work to pay for my trip to the city, moving lumber into piles. It was hard work. At night we couldn't sleep because the city was so noisy. We didn't wander far from the lumber yard for fear we wouldn't be able to find our way back. The smell of asphalt and oil and gas from the cars was almost overwhelming. It was like an ocean of cars. An ocean of lights. And an ocean of excitement. I never thought for a moment that before many years I would be back in that city studying music and from there God would move me around the world to witness for our Savior Jesus Christ.

I was only in Asuncion for a few days, but it was enough to let me know there were other things out in that world beyond the colony I'd grown up in. So a couple of years later, I was excited when my parents decided to move about 700 kilometres (430 miles) to a place called *Tres Palmas* in East Paraguay which is not in the *Chaco* but close to the *Iguazu* waterfalls, right on the Brazilian border – a long way from where I grew up. This colony was settled by Mennonites who had come from Manitoba in 1948.

Looking back, I can see that God could have had His hand in it, but money-wise I think we should have stayed where we were. By now, father had moved us from the native reservation back to the colony's capital of *Loma Plata*. All six of us boys were working, we couldn't afford to go to school. I was sixteen and still working at the cotton factory making quite a bit of money. Everything we made went directly to our parents so we could live. By then we had quite a nice house.

But Dad wanted to move. I suppose he was restless – we moved 22 times before I was 20 years old. And I think this was one of the reasons we were so terribly poor. The move they were planning would cost them everything they had made so far.

My Dad's mind was made up. One day we loaded all we could onto a big old truck, sold the rest, and set off – Mom and Dad with their six teenage sons. After many days of traveling we came to this beautiful place, a real tropical jungle paradise with lots of rivers. I loved the countryside. *Tres Palmas* had only 200 or 300 people but it seemed prosperous. Their main crops were soya beans and wheat. Many of the people in this area encouraged our family to start a new life. We were newcomers and these people didn't know what trouble-makers my brothers and I were supposed to be. In this new place we were real people with real feelings and we were respected among our new friends.

I got work in a carpentry shop and loved it. I made cabinets and that became a wonderful hobby for me. Soon I was foreman of one section. I got to know many different Christians. There was a wonderful group of young people in the church, I learned how to work with them, and I was having a great time.

And best of all, my Dad had bought me a Paraguayan harp! Some of the people in the colony had owned harps and for a few years I'd borrowed those as often as I could and tried to play. But now I had my very own harp — it was just a small one, old, and quite primitive. But oh, how I loved it, and the music I quickly learned to play on it. I handed my guitar to my brothers and spent every spare moment with my precious harp. A Christian radio station had begun broadcasting from one of the colonies and they played the same wonderful hymns I had heard from *HCJB* in Ecuador. I began playing along with them on my harp and it was just so beautiful. I was happy.

But my parents just couldn't make it there. My dad worked in construction and my mother milked cows for a ranch. As well, she made *empanadas* and sold them to the local people. My brothers, too, got work. But even so my parents said they couldn't make ends meet and after only 18 months decided to move back to the *Chaco*, to *Loma Plata*.

I couldn't believe it – move, move, move. We had all worked so hard in this new colony to make a new beginning for ourselves. And now, after such a short time they wanted to move again, 700 kilometres (430 mi.) back home. — I think they missed their family.

But I'd had it, I wasn't going back. "I'm staying here," I told them. And so they left me there, alone, but with amazing new friends, and I really enjoyed it.
My parents kept writing me letters that the colony and the *Chaco* had changed a lot. "Please, won't you come back?" they pleaded in letter after letter. They told me they'd made a new beginning there again, and I thought: "Great!" After three months I was feeling homesick too, and wanted to be with my brothers. So after

three months alone in *Tres Palmas*, I made my way back to my family in the *Chaco*. But when I got there, I could not believe my eyes. I had seen my parents poor many times before, but nothing like this. They had moved onto the main street where there were nice homes on both sides of the street. But the shed they were living in was about 6 by 6 metres (20 x 20 feet). It had big window openings but no screens to keep out the critters. They didn't even have an outhouse. There was maybe a metre (just over three feet) of tall grass around the house and in the grass they had dug a hole in the ground and placed a few planks across it. There were no walls or door, no privacy at all.

I was so ashamed – here I was an 18-year-old who had worked so hard to get things nice for my parents, and now I had to live in this. I had wanted to make an impression on the young people in town, but now they all made fun of us. We were the 'poor Klassens' still and I didn't like being so humiliated.

"We've got to smarten up," I said to my brothers. "We have to work hard enough to buy a decent house for our parents." And we did. We all started to work. I got a wonderful job in a carpentry shop just down the road and soon I was foreman there.

All our money went to purchase an old house with three rooms in it. It hadn't been lived in for a long time and was full of rats and mice. But compared to the shed we were living in, it was a mansion! We all worked hard to renovate it, and soon it became the beautiful place we called home for a long time. "The Klassen brothers" were still looked down on, but it didn't matter. God had blessed us and given us a beautiful place live.

# music!  the passion of my life!

After we moved into this house, some of the colony people saw that there was potential in those six Klassen brothers, that God had given us some gifts.  And I thank the Lord for those people who came to us in our poverty and asked us if we would use our gifts to praise God's Name among our people. They voted me to become a worker on the youth committee, helping especially in the music department.

Music had been the love of my life since I was seven years old when I first heard that wonderful music from *HCJB Radio* in Quito, Ecuador.  It changed my life forever. Night after night I listened to the music coming out of that little black box, and longed for a musical instrument so I could learn to play this music. But my parents couldn't afford it. Then, when I was about 12, I bought a guitar, and the native people taught me how to play it. I got my first harp when I was almost 17, and I'd been practicing and developing my own style.

*My first Harp Exam*

The leaders in our church saw I had a gift and invited me to be a part of the music in the church. By then, as well as guitars and harps, there were accordions and harmonicas among our group.  And they were allowing hymns in the church! I organized music programs and brought in nice music, especially instrumental. It was a lot of fun. Slowly I began to gain confidence that I could do something musically with my life even though I hadn't had the opportunity to study as much as some of the other young people in the colony.

We had about 300 young people getting together in the evenings, and we played music and games.  I organized youth retreats, and taught Sunday School lessons to youth and younger children, and I loved that too.  I had the opportunity to stand up in front of people and talk to them. And that gave me the confidence that maybe sometime in the future I might be on stage praising God.  So many dreams.

During the last couple of years that I lived at home, the colony opened up to the modern world very quickly when Mennonite missionaries came from Canada, the United States and Germany. They told us that church membership was not a highway to heaven, the only way to heaven was through Jesus Christ. Some held big evangelistic meetings, urging us to repent and accept Jesus as Savior. This was all new to us. I remember those amazing evenings, with hundreds of buggies parked around the church. Our people were hungry for the Word of God.

But at the same time, bad things were coming in. And I had a big hand in it. Somebody brought me a catalogue of music I could get from Germany, and I ordered rock music for our young people in the jungle. The music of AC/DC, KISS, the Rolling Stones, the Beatles, you name it. Some of it was music influenced by Satan, and with that music we were dancing around in the bush, we were smoking, and many of my friends were drinking alcohol.

*Aerial Photo of Loma Plata 2001*

So now it wasn't all rosy in the colony. Somehow we just didn't get it, that we needed to commit our lives to the Lord and determine to serve Him. The Lord spoke to me many times, that I should straighten out my life so He could use me in a mighty way one day. From listening to *HCJB* Christian radio all those years and then more recently to a Christian radio station in a neighboring colony, I knew there was a God who loved me even though I had done many bad things. I knew that Jesus Christ wanted to be Lord of my life. I was standing in front of young people and encouraging them to do the right things in life – yet I wasn't doing the right things myself.

But in 1980, a missionary was sent to our town by the Mennonite Central Committee of Canada to hold evangelistic meetings. And this time, at age twenty, I repented and was baptized. I truly believed I had become a child of God. I was determined to clean up all the dirt in my life, mostly the rock and roll music. I figured I could do it all by myself. But I held back in lot of areas, I wasn't ready to let Jesus Christ be boss of my life. There were a lot of things I held onto – secret things. Even though, along with my brothers, I'd said I wanted to walk in God's ways and was baptized, yet I carried on just the same as before, hiding my sins, pretending to be a good Christian Mennonite.

There was no real change in my life. I know now there should have been because *the Gospel of Jesus Christ changes lives*. The Bible says that *"When someone becomes a Christian, he becomes a brand new person inside. He is not the same anymore. A new life has begun." It says, "Christians no longer live to please themselves but instead they live to please Christ."* (2 Corinthians 5:17,15 TLB). Well, there sure was nothing new or different about Eduard Klassen. He was totally living to please himself. Nothing had changed in my life. I just kept on acting the way I thought a Christian should — when other people were watching..

*My Volleyball Team 1979*

*In Tres Palmas, 17 years*

# PART TWO –

# GOODBYE to my JUNGLE HOME!

*Dugout with grass in the Chaco*

*Natives Well*

*Lake in the Chaco*

# hello world! *Nine*

One day my church asked if they could send me to Asuncion to study music at the Mennonite seminary there, they offered some payment but mostly I would have to find a way to support myself. The missionary had told us young people that we should go to the city to study. And now I was being offered a chance to study music!  That appealed to me.

But my Mom and Dad were not too pleased at the thought of their oldest son leaving home.  But after many days of debating and praying about it, finally they said: "Eduard, you can go away to study with our blessing. But please promise us that when you are finished studying, you will move back to the colonies and live with us again." I promised – it's easy to promise when you're 20 years old and the world is opening up to you.

*Trans Chaco Highway*

And so I set off for the adventure of my life in the big city of Asuncion that I had visited five years earlier. My Mom and Dad were so sad to see me go, my Mom was crying. I walked away from my big close family, my friends, my church, my traditions. I moved to the big city with paved roads, electricity, running water, so many beautiful cars and beautiful homes. It seemed more awesome than five years earlier.
Again, I could hardly believe my eyes.

And what a challenge: I was going to have to learn how to live among modern people. I would have to learn Spanish really well because most classes were taught in that language (I knew a little, but barely enough to communicate).
And I would have to find a job that would pay my tuition.

I found my way to the Seminary and after a couple of hours went looking for an "outhouse". I wandered around the grounds and couldn't find one any-where, and I thought to myself, "Where do these fancy people go for stuff like that?"  Finally I asked one of the Spanish guys, "Where is the outhouse?"

*A* SOULFUL JOURNEY

He looked at me in disbelief, but finally understood that I meant business. "Follow me," he said." And I did. This guy walked into a building and inside he opened a door: "This is the washroom." I looked into that fancy tiled room and saw six or seven white thrones in a row. I thought they were the most beautiful things I'd seen in my life! This guy must have understood that I had no clue what I was looking at, he was so good to me and explained how these 'thrones' worked. And then, bless him, he left me alone.

When I flushed the toilet, the noise was so loud I jumped back about five metres and stood in a corner, thinking to myself — "Man alive, I am so stupid! Twenty years old and I don't know how to use a modern toilet! What comes next?"

What came next was a bright shiny box sitting on a table, they said it was a telephone. I had no idea how it worked, I couldn't believe it when they said I could talk all the way to Canada on it!

I didn't want these fancy city people to know I didn't know how to use a telephone. So one day I decided to telephone my friend Peter who also had come from the Colony to Asuncion to study. Some students were sitting around watching what would happen next. I dialed the number, then picked up the phone. All I heard was a buzzing noise.

*Concert in Loma Plata 1989*

But I wasn't going to make a fool of myself in front of all those people so I said, "How are you doing Peter, could you please pick me up at 3 o'clock." I hung up the phone and smugly walked out of the room. But everyone there knew I hadn't talked to Peter because you have to pick up the phone before you dial the number.

When I left the jungle I could barely read or write, and only in High German. I finished Grade 6 and then had to go to work. So at seminary I found I had to study really hard, first on my Spanish so I could begin to understand what was being said in class. There were many times I thought I'd never make it through the first semester.

I was enrolled in a music program and one day in class the instructor asked: "Eduard, could you please give us Middle C."

I hadn't a clue what he was talking about, I had seen a piano once but had no idea how it worked. But the professor turned to the big box at the front. Again, I didn't want to make a fool of myself in front of my fellow students so I walked up to that box, lined up the keys and hit the middle one. And that was my luckiest day ever in my music ministry – I hit Middle C dead on!  Can you imagine, the little boy from a mud house in the Paraguayan jungle got it right!  Wow! How much my Lord and God has blessed me, how much He has changed my life around.

I didn't want my city friends to know I'd come from a mud house in a poor community, so I lied to them many times.  Now I'm not ashamed of my background because I know that God can use one of the poorest of this world, God can prepare someone even from a little mud house in the Paraguayan jungle, to serve Him all over the world.

But it was not easy to get used to living in a city with paved roads, electricity, cars, and amazing buildings with running water and flush toilets. So many people in our modern country take things like that for granted. Yet there are millions of people in this world who will never see or experience what you and I have every single day. We must never forget to thank God that He lets us live in this wonderful place.

– ◆ –

Now when I went to the South American Theological Seminary, I thought I had given my life to Christ – but I hadn't given up everything. I was still smoking, secretly.  At one point I had given it up for a few months but started again.  If I had been caught they could have kicked me out of the seminary and that would have been a huge humiliation for me.  (I thank the Lord that He eventually helped me beat that bad habit — but that is a story for later.)

Before I came to Asuncion, the only church I had known was our Old Colony German Mennonite Church, held in a nice but very plain brick house, where the service for most of my years there was very serious and the singing only monotonous Gregorian chants.  Just before I left home the missionaries had taught us some of the newer hymns.  But on the whole, for a young person our church had been very dull and boring.

So can you imagine my amazement the first time I walked into a Spanish Church and saw the people standing, clapping, smiling, singing,  some of them were even dancing down the aisles with their hands up! Wow! When I saw that, I said to my friend, (another boy from the colonies): "Hey, we'd better watch what we're doing – these people are all nuts!"

But I soon realized that these Spanish brothers and sisters had not come to church just to sleep or to warm up the church benches like I'd done all my life. These people were excited and praising the Lord from the bottom of their hearts. And I had thought that we Germans were the only people who would make it into Heaven! It was an astonishing revelation that began transforming my life. I couldn't get enough of this wonderful happy music, and these people who were on fire for the Lord.

I worked so hard in the city to learn what I had missed while living out in the jungle all those years. It was not easy for me to leave my family and friends and come to this strange new culture. I praise Him every single day that He touched my heart through missionary radio as a little child in my little mud-brick jungle home, and for the missionaries who told us that we should repent and accept Jesus as our Savior. Thanks be to God that He had brought me from the jungle to a place where I could study and prepare for the wonderful life God had in store for me.

# the world opens up to me

During those five years at the Seminary I worked as a cashier at a food market to pay my way. In addition to theology, I studied music. I couldn't learn the harp as my major instrument because it was not an instrument on their curriculum, so I studied piano at the Seminary and took harp lessons on the side. I earned enough money to buy a lovely, traditional Paraguayan harp, patterned after the classical harps the first Spanish missionaries brought to South America. The Paraguayan harp is made of thin cedar and pine wood so is much lighter weight than the European harp. It has only five octaves and no foot pedals so the playing is somewhat limited.

*My first Tour in Germany*

But this lovely harp was the joy of my life. For over five years I studied privately with one of the best Paraguayan harpists who taught me to play the native Paraguayan style. Because I had taught myself in the jungle I was using all the wrong hand positions, so he had to teach me all over again. At that point it was just a hobby instrument, but I loved that harp, and I guess it showed.

In 1985 I had just finished studying music when an evangelist came from Germany to Paraguay, and I was asked to play the harp in his services. I played the old hymns and the evangelist loved the music so much that he gave his business card to me with the invitation: "Eduard, anytime you want to come to Germany to play your harp and tour with me, just call or write me."

I thanked him, shoved the card in my pocket and forgot about it. Months later I was going through the stuff in my drawer and came across this card again. "Hey," I said to my friends, "isn't this amazing! I think I'll try it." So I wrote the evangelist a letter saying that if he was still interested in having me there, I'd love to come.

In no time I received a letter back – Yes, his team would like me to come. "And we want you to bring two others with you to make a music team," the letter said. "We'll pay all expenses for you and your team." Wow! That wouldn't be hard to arrange.

Three months later, three guys from the jungle were sitting at the International Airport in Asuncion, tickets in hand, on their way to the modern country of Germany! One was a wonderful pianist, Dario Frutos, a Baptist with Spanish background, the other was accordionist Siegfried Siemens, a Mennonite from a different colony. And Eduard with his harp. We were all single — and looking!

By now I was 25-years-old, and for the first time I was boarding a big jumbo jet.
A nice young lady came by and told us to "Buckle up". We didn't have a clue what she was talking about. When she came by a third time and found us just sitting there she was annoyed: "You guys buckle up right now." But I was frustrated: " Lady, I am buckled up already," I told her, lifting my shirt and pointing to my belt. She soon set us straight.

*My first trip to Germany in 1985*

As I settled into a soft, luxurious seat I was wondering to myself: Could this be the plane I had seen and shot at with my sling-shot so many times when I was a little boy looking into the sky from my jungle home? I had never dreamed so many people could fit into a big bird like this. I never dreamed I would have the chance to find out. But here I was, 'buckled up', ready to fly. It was totally amazing.

I had the window seat, and after a long flight, as we came down through the clouds over Frankfurt, Germany, I woke up my friends: "Guys, look outside, they have white dirt in Germany." It was December, and when we touched down that 'white dirt' went flying all over the place. Finally the plane stopped.

When we walked into the airport, a bunch of young people were waiting for us. "Welcome to Germany!" they greeted us. "You're lucky we have a lot of snow outside today." SNOW! We'd heard about snow but had never seen it. We rushed outside and began scooping up that beautiful white stuff, rubbing it onto our faces, putting it in our pockets – just amazing! But soon we learned it melts and is just as wet as water!

The German young people took us to their big car and we piled into the back seat. And we were off, flying down that Autobahn at 180 kilometres (110 miles) an hour. "Slow down, guys!" we yelled.  But they didn't understand our mix of Spanish and Low German. Why are they going so fast? we wondered. One of these young people was Waldemar Neufeld who has booked five tours for us in Germany since that time.  Waldemar and his wife Maria have become good friends.

We stayed at the evangelist's home for a couple of days preparing for our European tour – the first tour ever for me. Before starting out, the evangelist bought all three of us brand new suits, those were the most beautiful clothes I had ever worn in my life.

That tour was an eye-opener I will never forget.  I think I learned more in that one trip than in all my years of study- ing.  I learned how to deal with people, and how to stand on a concert platform in front of thousands of sophisticated Europeans and play music. This was NOT Paraguay for sure!  After three months of traveling in Europe, I felt a call from the Lord that this was the ministry He wanted me to spend my life doing. But I didn't know how or where.

*The first snow I ever saw*

We returned to Asuncion where I again got work and continued my studies. During the next few years, I was invited twice more to tour with the German evangelist, just me and my harp.

– ◆ –

Now it so happened that a couple of months before my first trip to Germany, my friend Ed Neufeld had casually asked: "Eduard, aren't your Mom and Dad Canadians?" I replied "No".

"How about your grandparents, your great-grandparents?" Yes, they were all born in Canada.

And then he came up with an incredible idea: "Eduard, I think I can get you Canadian Citizenship!"

I wasn't really interested in looking into citizenship until Ed explained: "Canadian Citizenship  means that with those papers you could go to Canada and live there. I'll help you, it won't cost much money," he offered.

I was so excited – now I would have a chance to see the country my grandparents and great grandparents left so many years ago.

Ed also helped me get a Canadian Passport – now I could really go.  I wrote to my mom and dad out in the *Chaco* to tell them I was going "really home", not back to their jungle but to our true family home in Manitoba, Canada.

*Dario, Eduard, Siegfried in Germany*

*A Concert in Bielefeld, Germany*

# CANADA – my new home!

On May 15th, 1986 I left the 38°C (100.4 F) of Asuncion, boarded a jumbo jet and headed for the 'frozen north'. I was traveling with my friend Rudy who had also managed to get Canadian Citizenship and Passport. We landed first in Miami. I remember stepping out of the plane into that awesome airport. Neither of us could speak or read any English, we just followed the crowd and found ourselves at U.S. Customs. We were standing in line, both of us holding our Canadian passports, trying not to look as scared as we felt about the whole procedure around us. We were so unsure, we didn't know how to behave.

*My First Concert in Canada at the Steinbach Museum*

Finally it was our turn and there was a very nice looking African-American lady standing behind the counter. We stared at her! We'd never seen a black person in South America, we might have seen one in Germany. But we certainly had never talked to a black person face to face. We couldn't take our eyes off her. She had an amazing smile, with dazzling white teeth –
I remember it to this day.

We handed our passports to this lady. With a big smile on her face, she talked about fifty miles (80km) an hour. We couldn't understand one word she said, we just looked at her and nodded our heads. She stamped the passports and in a few minutes we were done. She smiled again, and waved her hand towards the door we should go through to catch our plane to Canada.

Now I wanted to impress this lady, she was so nice. So I said to my friend, "Wait a minute!" I turned to this nice lady and said the only English words I knew: "Yes, sir!"

You should have seen the change on her face! Now she began talking twice as fast — 100 miles (160 km) an hour, and although I couldn't understand a word she was saying I knew she was not happy! We escaped through that door, and later I learned that you don't say "Yes sir" to a woman! I learned I would have to be careful what I said because it could mean something quite different from what I thought.

*A* SOULFUL JOURNEY

We walked onto the plane and flew to Canada, landing in Winnipeg, Manitoba. My cousin, Arthur Klassen, met us; he'd paid for my ticket to come to Canada. Cousin Arthur had moved to Winnipeg four years earlier, and I stayed with them until I could afford to rent an apartment with Rudy.

I was so proud to be in the country my great-grandparents had left almost 60 years earlier. I thought I'd stay a year and just check it out because I was a Canadian citizen.

It was awesome to live in this modern country, I'd never dreamed of such a privilege, and soon I had no wish to leave. I got a job in a carpentry shop, Kitchencraft Cabinets.

They gave me a lot of money for working for them — $5.35 an hour! I'd never seen that much money in my whole life. I was enjoying myself. Rudy and I made friends with other young guys we'd grown up with in Paraguay, who had moved to Canada earlier. There were about 2000 Paraguayan Mennonites living in Winnipeg at that time including my boss at the carpentry shop and almost 50 other employees. After working there for six weeks, I found a job with almost twice the pay in a unionized shop, Builder's Furniture.

*My First Car in Canada 1987*

When August came, my boss closed the shop for two weeks, for holidays! I'd never had holidays in my life. I sure wasn't going to sit around for two weeks. I announced to my friends: "I'm going downtown and buy myself a train ticket!"

I'd never had a train ride. I was so excited about it because my great-grandparents, years ago when I was little, had talked about the wonderful train ride they had from Winnipeg to New York before they took the ship to South America.

I had $240 in my pocket – that was amazing! In only three months I had paid for my flight to Canada, I'd been buying food and paying my rent. And I had all that money left in my pocket. Surely I was the richest single guy in Canada! I bought a train ticket to Vancouver, BC, it cost $168 return. I had cousins there. I couldn't speak English yet, I hadn't bothered to learn because all my friends and the guys in the shop spoke German or Spanish.

I walked into that train station and onto that beautiful train and had the trip of my life, through the Prairies, through the Rockies, and on to Vancouver, BC. My cousin and some of his friends picked me up and I stayed with this cousin in Vancouver for several days.

At that time the Vancouver EXPO was on, like a World's Fair. When I went to EXPO with these friends in the evening it was like paradise on earth – so many lights, so many rides – a fairyland! But I had no idea what these young people had prepared for me. A nice looking girl from the group asked me if I would go with her on a little train. Of course I would. "Are you sure?" she asked again.

I turned to her: "Lady, don't you know I came from Winnipeg on a big CP train towing 20 wagons behind. For two days and two nights I was sitting in that big train. This little thing is nothing, it can't hurt a fly," I boasted.

"Eduard," she said, "have you ever heard about a roller coaster?" No, I admitted.

"Would you like to try it with me?" With that nice lady, why not?

I remember stepping into the little train. Then we went up a ramp slowly, ticka, ticka, ticka, ticka. She was talking, we were looking out over the lights of EXPO in that beautiful Vancouver night. Beautiful lights in a beautiful sky and a beautiful young lady beside me. I think it was the most romantic 30 seconds of my life! "Man alive, this is an amazing trip," I thought.

But as we came closer to the top of the ramp, the nice lady beside me quit talking. "Oh, oh, she's afraid of heights," I thought. But when we got to the very top, there was a pause, we sort of hung there, and then –whoosh! The crazy train went straight down. Straight down into the black Vancouver night! People all around were yelling and screaming. My body was flying down into that black hole but I don't know where my soul was. It hurt so much I couldn't even scream. When the first curve came it hurt even more. And then we started climbing again, and down again, around another curve again. And the woman beside me was yelling her lungs off. I thought, "This is it, these are the last seconds of my life and then I will be dead."

But when this crazy little train stopped, I didn't hear the voices in heaven, instead I heard my cousins and their friends yelling and screaming, "Eduard, welcome to Canada!"

Yes, right – that night I learned what a roller coast is and I'll never forget it. I've been on a roller coaster since, but now I know what's coming up around the next corner, and at the top of the ramp it goes straight down and really hurts!

Back in Winnipeg, one December day winter arrived and I couldn't believe it! I never thought this world could be so cold. Sure, we'd had winter snow in Germany, but the - 42°C of Winnipeg was unbelievable. Especially for a boy who grew up where 40°C (104 F) was the norm. And it stayed that cold for two weeks!

*Ready for a Concert in Winnipeg 1992*

Now I knew exactly why my great-grandparents had moved away from this bitterly cold Canada. It was so cold, I couldn't put enough jackets around me. I thought I would die when I went outside, the - 42°C really burns your face. It was colder than any refrigerator I'd seen in Paraguay!

After a long long winter in that freezing Winnipeg icebox, spring finally came to the Prairies. It was a beautiful country. I traveled down to where my great-grandparents had had their farm, it was wonderful to see this part of my history.

My dear brothers and sisters, my dear friends in Canada, we have the privilege of living in one of the most beautiful countries in this world, and we have to thank our Lord and Savior every day for this. We take it all for granted while there are millions of people who would love to see it, but never will. Yet we know this country is nothing compared to what is to come because there's a beautiful Heaven waiting for us. Heaven may come sooner than we think so let's be on fire for our Lord. Not just pastors, not just missionaries – God wants you and me to be on fire, talking about our Lord and Savior who died for our sins so that you and I can be saved. It is awesome to be a Christian, but it is also absolutely wonderful to serve God with the gifts He has given to us. Let's be excited about it and tell the rest of the world what the Lord has done for us.

– ◆ –

# travels with my singing harp

I was enjoying my work at the Winnipeg carpentry shop. And I had my harp. I played it in the church I was attending, and soon I was being invited to play at other churches. I couldn't understand why people in Canada liked it so much when I played the old hymns. But I loved sharing in their services. And they paid me – soon I was making more money playing my harp than working as a carpenter. One day I said to my friends: "You know what? I think God is calling me to play the harp full-time." It made sense to me that when the ministry was prospering so much, it must be what God wanted me to do.

*Concert in Indiana, USA*

But I didn't speak any English. Usually I could make it through a concert without saying much, I just stood there and played for an hour and fifteen minutes, no problem. Yet I knew if I went on tour, I would have to learn English – fast. On the other hand, all of the churches inviting me were Mennonite and some had German services so I was O.K. for a little while.

For my previous tours in Germany, not only did I know the language, but the evangelist had arranged all the concerts for me. Where would I start in Canada? How could I contact the different churches? I was going to have to figure this out on my own.

I had many friends in the Winnipeg area although they were German or Spanish. Yet I wanted so badly to make a tour of Western Canada, how could I make contacts?

Then someone gave me a newspaper, *"Die Mennonitische Post"*, and in it there were addresses in Regina, Saskatoon, Edmonton, and Swift Current. One caught my eye – a Mrs. Giesbrecht in Swift Current. Surely she must be a German-speaking person, I thought. So I telephoned the number listed. "Hello, Mrs. Giesbrecht, I am Eduard Klassen living in Winnipeg but I am a Mennonite from Paraguay, South America." Praise the Lord, she answered in Low German, just like me!

A SOULFUL JOURNEY

"I am quite sure you go to a Mennonite Church," I said. And she answered, yes, she did and I could tell she was quite interested because she had heard about the Paraguay Mennonites. She was 82-years-old and very friendly. So I was encouraged to ask: "Mrs. Geisbrecht, I am a harpist and I play the beautiful old hymns on my harp. I've been on tour in Germany, now I would like to play my music in Canadian churches. Would you be willing to ask your pastor if I could come to your church and play music there? "

And believe it or not, this dear lady was so good to me, she asked her pastor if I could come and give a concert in their church! And he was so good too, he said "Yes, come and play."

But now I got nervous – I didn't want to go alone, and I had no back-up music. What would I do? So I wrote to my friend who had played the accordion with me on tour in Germany, Siegfied Siemens. I paid his ticket to fly from Paraguay to go with me on my first Western Canada Tour. I had one concert booked, but I was sure there would be others.

*Concert in Jamaica 2003*

And sure enough, it happened. In Swift Current, Saskatchewan, we played our first concert and the people loved it. They encouraged us so much. Mrs. Giesbrecht had lots of friends all over Canada; she got in touch with them and they invited us to their churches. The pastor called some other churches too. We would drive to a town and give a concert, the people who attended would talk about it and urge their pastors to invite us and that would open doors for other concerts. We played in many nursing and retirement homes and that helped spread the word. Soon we were booked solid. It kept us very busy traveling from church to church, through Saskatchewan, Alberta and British Columbia – we had 32 concerts that first tour!

Even though we didn't know the language and the culture of this new country, God can do wonderful things. I had written out my testimony in High German and a friend had translated it into English for me. I read that to the people at the concerts. But after doing a concert at the Mennonite Brethren Church in Coaldale, Alberta, somehow I left my testimony on the pulpit and drove off to the next town. What would I do? There was no time to rewrite and translate it – I was stuck. I had to do it from memory. From then on, I began to talk more and more on stage. And if you ever attended one of my early concerts, between then and now I hope you can see a huge change. In many ways.

The next year I paid for my brother Gustav to come to Canada to go on tour with me. He was a very fine classical guitarist, and the people loved the music of these two boys from the jungles of Paraguay. We had a great time traveling together, playing in so many beautiful churches and towns, and sometimes on television. We were both so limited in the English language that we could hardly say yes or no. Yet God looked after us so wonderfully, opening doors for us, blessing us and providing for our every need.

I remember coming home to my apartment in Winnipeg late one night, exhausted after a tour through Western Canada. Gustav and I were both half asleep and went straight to bed. In the morning Gustav came to me and said: "Eduard, I've lost my tie." You must understand that at that time, a tie was a lot of money for us. I tried to calm him down, "Don't worry, Gustav, I'll ask the caretaker if she found it when she was cleaning the apartment building this morning."

*Concert in Germany*

I didn't know how to say "tie" in English so I got out my dictionary and looked up the word. I found "tie", put my finger right on it, dialed the caretaker's number, and in my terrible, broken English said: "Hi, this is Eduard Klassen in 209."

"You are who?" she asked.

By this time I was scared to say it again, I knew my accent wasn't helping because she was not understanding me. But I tried again: "I am Eduard Klassen from 209."

This time she got it: "Yes, yes, what do you want?" she asked.

By now I was nervous and shaking, and must have moved my finger a little bit from the word, so I said, "I think my brother lost his *tire* in the building."

"Don't joke around with me," she shot back angrily.
"No, no, I 'm not joking, it's serious," and again I told her my brother had lost his tire.

By this time the lady is fuming on the other end of the line: "Is it a big one or a small one?" she demanded.

"A big one, he's a big guy," I told her.

Going along with me, she asked, "Mr. Klassen, where did your brother have his tire?"

I responded: "In his pocket."

By this time she was so upset I decided I'd better go down to talk to her face to face, so I could explain with my hands what I was talking about. That day I learned how to say "tie" and "tire" and the big difference between them! There were so many times when I could barely communicate what I was thinking, but God helped me through those times. It's not easy living in a foreign country, learning another language and another culture. I thank God that I finally learned to communicate in English.

However, in those early days of touring, when Gustav and I were alone we spoke the Low German we had grown up with. Sometimes this got us into trouble, like the time we were on tour in the Midwest and decided to go shopping, my brother badly needed some new clothes. We came to a big department store with the name "SEARS" on the front. Inside were so many beautiful things. "Gustav,' I said, "today is your day, I will pay for whatever you need." But as soon as I said that, I was sorry because I knew he would probably find the most expensive stuff in the store.

He was looking first for a T-shirt but couldn't find anything he liked. A nice looking lady appeared and with a big smile on her face asked: "Can I help you gentlemen with anything?"

"Oh sure," I said in broken English, adding, "My brother needs a T-shirt."

"No problem, I'll help you find one." She began looking through a rack and pulled out a brightly colored shirt. "How about this one?"

My brother didn't like it, and in Low German said to me: "Eduard, I would never buy such a crazy green shirt from this woman!"

This lady turned around and with a big grin answered in Low German!
"OK, guys, let's look for another one."

We were so embarrassed and ashamed, we must have turned every color. I could have melted away like a piece of hot butter on the floor. I didn't know what to do.

We'd been so rude to this nice lady who was trying to help us, and we just put her down. Even when she understood what we were saying, she was still nice to us. It was a lesson I've never forgotten, that we need to live our lives transparently, not hiding anything, not saying bad things about a person around the corner where we think they can't hear us. God hears. He sees and knows. Let's be honest at all times, because the Bible says we are to be an "open letter" to the rest of the world.

# PART THREE –

# GOD TURNS MY LIFE AROUND

## ...totally!

*Flowers in the Chaco*

*Our Engagement 1991*

*Concert in Kansas, USA*

# found out! ...

Chapter Thirteen

Yes, God's Word says we should be an "open letter" at all times. But the truth was, I was far from that. I was not living transparently. I had sin in my life that I was hiding from people.

One of the biggest things was that I was still smoking. Smoking may not be a sin for some people, but for me it was and God kept telling me I should stop. Sure, I tried to quit but went right back to it, chewing gum all the time and wearing lots of cologne so people wouldn't smell tobacco smoke on me. It shamed me to be sharing the gospel on stage while I had not cleaned up my own life. I was lying to myself and being dishonest with others.
I felt so guilty.

For almost three years it was like that while I toured throughout Canada, the USA and Europe. And then one day in November, 1990, it all came home to me. I had just finished a long tour in Europe and was in the Frankfurt airport waiting for my boarding call. And I thought: "Now I'm away from all those Christians I'll have a cigarette." So I lit up.

And as I'm standing there, thinking I'm all alone and far from home, who should come up to me but a man from my home church in Winnipeg! In shock he asked: "Eduard, are you a smoker?"
Oh oh, this is it, I thought, now the whole world will know what a hypocrite I've been.

Quickly I stubbed out the cigarette and stammered: "I'm not really a smoker, it's just that I'm nervous and I've been told a cigarette would calm me." With a sick heart I knew he wouldn't believe me. My ministry was finished, I figured.

All the way home my heart was like a heavy stone choking me. God spoke to me so clearly: "Eduard Klassen, you know you are a phony, a big hypocrite. It's time to get real."

Oh yes, dear brothers and sisters, I was a hypocrite. The 'testimony' I'd written down on paper was just empty, empty. The Holy Spirit had knocked on the door of my heart many, many times. Down in the jungle when just a little boy I listened to that little black box and from missionary radio *HCJB* Ecuador I'd heard that God loves me, and sent Jesus to die for me to save me from my sins and take me to heaven. Mennonite missionaries had come to the jungle and told me that church membership was not a ticket to heaven. They told us we couldn't work hard enough to work our way into heaven, it was only by the grace of Jesus Christ and what He had done for us on the Cross that we could be saved. They urged us to repent and accept Jesus Christ as Savior. And I went through the motions of doing that, and was baptized.

But when I went to the big city to study, I was the biggest hypocrite you could have found. I began to question many things: "Is God really there? Are the Mennonites the only ones who are good? Are all the Baptists and Presbyterians lost?"

For these past three years I'd been travelling the world playing my harp and praying that God would bless the concerts. I read my Bible almost every day. Yet as I flew home over that wide ocean, I knew I had so much sin in my life. Sins that I loved more than anything or anyone else. Smoking was only one of them, there were others, bigger sins. I was such a liar. And I was so full of fear. Sometimes I woke up at night, having just dreamed that I had died and landed in hell and couldn't get out, I'd just burn and burn forever and ever. I'd be shaking, it was awful.

All those years I had tried so hard to live the Christian life. I tried to clean up my life. I tried to get rid of my sins. But I couldn't do it. All the time God's Holy Spirit had been coming to me, softly and tenderly touching my heart, saying, "Eduard, why don't you come to the Cross and dump your sin right there?" Stubbornly, I just kept on trying to get rid of it by myself.

But that night on the aircraft, that mountain of sin was so big and heavy I knew I couldn't carry it any longer. I was so sick of all the lying and pretending. I wanted to be free from being a slave to sin. I was desperate. As soon as I got home to my apartment in Winnipeg, I fell on my knees and began to cry and beg: "Oh God, please help me! I can't go on like this anymore. I'm such a miserable sinner. I've made such a mess of my life. I've got to get rid of all this sin. Please, please, take away my sins. Come into my heart and set me free! I want to be the man you want me to be. I'm ready to do whatever you ask. I want to serve you with a pure heart."

For the first time I began really talking to God. For the first time I really meant business. And I told Him, "Even if it takes days or weeks, I'm staying here until I know for sure that You've taken away all my sins and made me Your child."

But it didn't take days or weeks. There on my knees I opened my Bible to John 3:16 - 21 and started to read: *"God loved the world so much that He gave His only Son so that anyone who believes in Him shall not perish but have eternal life."* And it was as if Jesus Christ was right in that room speaking those words to me. He reminded me of how many times He'd spoken to my heart. He showed me the way He'd led me and cared for me through all those years. That night I came to the end of a long highway, and broke in the presence of our awesome God. For two hours I cried and confessed my sins.

And after two hours I knew, I knew for sure that God had forgiven my sins and made me His child. I knew at 12:35 p.m. November 27th, 1990, that my Lord and Savior Jesus Christ had come in and taken over my heart and my life. I was truly a free man! All the fear was gone. I felt a peace and joy like never before.

It was wonderful, the most amazing moment of my life! I was thirty years old.

I took my pack of cigarettes and wrote on it: "This is my last pack. This is the day of my total commitment to serve Jesus Christ and live as His child should." I went to bed and slept like a baby with no fears, no bad dreams.

Over the next months I lost many friends. It didn't take long for word to get around: "Something has happened to Eduard Klassen. The guy is so happy, and he says he's quit smoking. But that won't last, he'll be smoking again tomorrow just like he always has every other time he's tried to quit," they taunted.

But it did last, I never smoked another cigarette. God totally delivered me that day I was "born again" into His family. He made me a brand new person inside and out. And now all I want to do is live my life to please my Lord and Savior Jesus Christ. Now He truly is boss of my life. I'm just the servant, I take my orders for each day from Him. Someone said, "If Christ is not Lord of all, He's not Lord at all." That was true for me.

And my dear friends, maybe you too went through the motions of becoming a Christian, but nothing in your life changed. Maybe it's because you, just like me, never truly made Jesus Christ the boss of your life. Dear friends, if you don't know for sure that you've had all your sins washed away and been born into God's family, I urge you right now to get on your knees and mean business with God. Open your Bible to John 3:16 and let Him speak to your heart, the same as He spoke so clearly to my heart. And just like He did for me, He'll take away all your load of sin and fear, and fill your heart and life with peace and joy and love. Please, please, don't wait another minute!

I know now it was no accident that a man from my home church walked up to me in Frankfurt airport and made me face up to my sins and brought me to the end of my rope. God was in that. He loved me so much, and wanted me to be happy and free and part of His family. And He wants that for you too.

– ◆ –

# god gives me a new family

As I said, the day I made Jesus Christ the Lord of my life and totally committed everything to Him, I lost many friends. But God gave me many new ones, including my beautiful wife, Christine. Just three months later I saw her for the first time. It happened this way.....

My brother Gustav with his guitar, and I with my harp were on tour in Ontario.  Gustav had also become truly 'born again', and he too was a brand new person in Jesus Christ.

We were enjoying touring and witnessing for our Lord as never before.  It really was great!

One night we had a concert booked for Tavistock Mennonite Church.  In the middle of the concert my brother leaned over and whispered: "Eduard, do you see the two blonde girls sitting there?" Yes, I'd seen them, and couldn't believe that my brother would talk like that on stage. One of those blonde girls was the one I would marry. But of course I didn't know that then.

*Concert in Paraguay*

We met after the program when some of the young people got together for coffee.  Christine lived in Stratford, Ontario, just twenty minutes from the little motel where Gustav and I were staying. A couple of weeks later we were invited to have supper with another group of young people. I discovered Christine would be there. "We'll make a Paraguayan meal!" I offered.

That day, Gustav and I were in a Kitchener recording studio taping two 30-minute TV programs.  But it took the whole day and we arrived late for supper.  And in our hurry  I burned the '*giso*' – a rice dish with meat and tomato sauce. So much for making an impression on Christine!  Still, we got to know each other a little better. And then I went home to Winnipeg.

*Engagement 1991*

I hadn't told Christine I was interested in her.  She was working full-time as a Registered Nurse.  But I knew that in September she would be coming to

Winnipeg Bible College for a one-year course, and I could hardly wait!
I wrote her a letter telling her what a good time I'd had with her. I checked it with
my computer 'Spell-check' and all seemed OK. But Christine didn't know what to think
when she read Eduard had had a 'god' time with her. Finally she arrived in
Winnipeg and we began dating and I was on a cloud. In the spring of 1992 Christine
finished Bible College and returned to Ontario. In August, 1992 we were married
and made our home in Stratford, Ontario.

I wanted to show my new wife where I was born and raised. So in early 1993,
Christine and I flew to Miami and then on to Asuncion, Paraguay. It was interesting
seeing everything through Christine's eyes. My brother Wilfried picked us up in his van,
he was a pastor now in the capital city. While we were driving from the airport, a
donkey ran down the road ahead of us and we couldn't get past. He stayed there a
long time and we just had to poke along. "Welcome to Paraguay!" we told
Christine.

*Palm trees in the Chaco*

Before driving out to the *Chaco* we stayed with my brother
for a few days. "I want to show you one of the happiest
couples I've ever met in my life," Wilfried told us. And
he drove us to a jungle area outside the city. We came to
a little shed that was hardly more than a lean-to. Wilfried
knocked on the door and someone called out
a cheery "Come in."

In that one little room there were two beds, the husband
lay on one and his wife on the other. They were about 80
years old. Everything was so primitive. There were two
empty fish cans that they used to eat and drink out of, and only one spoon hanging
above their fire just to try to keep it a little bit clean. There was one pot to cook
their one meal each day which was usually *mandioke or cassava,* a root similar to
potatoes except a lot drier.

With big smiles they sat on the edges of their beds and told us their story.
They were both victims of leprosy, both had no fingers, the wife had lost one foot.
They told us how many years ago when they were sick with leprosy and shunned
by everyone in their village, they were sitting by their river waiting to die, when
down the river came a canoe, with white missionaries in it. "They stopped and
spoke to us, they touched us, they put us in their canoe and took us to a leprosy

clinic where we lived for many years. "The nurses and doctors looked after us and God healed us from this dreadful disease. But the best thing they did for us was tell us about Jesus, and we accepted Him as our personal Savior. We have suffered so long, but praise God, soon we are going to the Golden City Jesus is preparing for us. We won't suffer any more, and we'll live there with other children of God, in eternity forever and ever!"

This dear couple deeply touched my heart. They didn't know they were poor, they were just rejoicing in their salvation, and the hope of soon being with Jesus in heaven. I remembered that I didn't know we were poor when I was living in such poverty in our mud-brick jungle home. My parents loved us and we knew they would never let us down. What more could a child ask for?

As I write now, many years later, I know this old couple have gone to be with their Lord. It could be you or me next – are we ready to meet Jesus?

Christine and I drove the 500 kilometres (370 miles) into the jungle where I had lived the first 20 years of my life. Now we drove on paved highway, except for the last 20 kilometres (12 miles) which was still a mud track through the jungle. The heat was excruciating and the bugs were everywhere – that hadn't changed!

But much had changed in the *Chaco* since I left. There were about 9000 Mennonites in the colony, and almost half had become truly born-again, genuine believers, thanks to Mennonite missionaries coming in from Canada, the States, Europe, Argentina and Brazil. Yes, there are still many nominal Mennonites who are not thankful for what they have and what God has done for them. But most of the pastors are preaching the gospel of salvation by faith in Jesus Christ and many Mennonites have become evangelical and are going throughout Paraguay bringing the gospel to remote areas.

*My mother's home in 1995 with impending storm*

My parents had changed too – in 1983 they came to know Jesus Christ as their very own Savior – it was wonderful to see the difference in the way they were living, in so many ways.

*A* SOULFUL JOURNEY

They'd changed houses since I was there. It was much nicer, but still mud-brick, with an out-house in the yard. But there was an indoor toilet of sorts with a water tank on the roof, and a chain beside the toilet to pull for flushing. Christine was thankful for this, especially when I showed her the out-house with gross frogs and snakes down the hole, and huge poisonous spiders hiding under the toilet seat. One of my friends was bitten by one of those spiders just before he was married and it made him sterile. Not a good idea....

My poor bride Christine, there were so many bugs everywhere. And frogs. The first time Christine took a shower she came flying out fast – the walls were covered with little frogs and as soon as she turned the water on they all headed for it, could they ever jump! They freaked her out.

Thankfully, the straw mattresses had been replaced by foam and was I ever glad. How I hated those old flour bags stuffed with dry grass that we slept on as kids. They were so noisy, and full of blood-sucking roaches.

There was only one room with an air-conditioner – an old thing as loud as a bulldozer. But it kept us from sweating in the awful heat, so we shared the room for sleeping with my parents. There were two beds of course. In the middle of the night Christine woke up screaming: "Eduard, there's a bug in my ear!"

"Lie on your pillow and I'll pour water into your ear, " I told her. And out floated the biggest bug I'd ever seen. My Mom and Dad just kept snoring away, they didn't know a thing. All this must have been very hard for my dear wife, especially with her training as a registered nurse in our nice sterile Canadian hospitals.

I played a concert in the church there in the *Chaco,* and the people really enjoyed the old hymns and folks songs played on my lovely Paraguayan harp.

– ◆ –

*Our Wedding Picture*

*Mathias and Eduard at concert in Mississippi*

# a chance to give back…
## "What a mighty God we serve!"

After five weeks Christine and I returned to Canada and began our life of touring and ministering together. Soon we were performing up to 250 concerts a year, sometimes in front of thousands of people, other times just a few. I've played in churches of many different denominations, in colleges, concert halls, and on radio and television programs. And sometimes I play for an audience all dressed in orange;– in other words, people in jail clothes. I count that a special privilege because I get a chance to witness to those who really are at the end of their highway. And just as in other concerts, many have accepted Jesus Christ as Savior and Lord through hearing the sweet old gospel hymns, and my testimony of what God has done in my life.

*Mom and Dad 1997*

We have never charged for any concert, we always go on a freewill offering basis or honorarium. Wherever the doors are open I go — on one condition, that I can share my faith story — my testimony — with others. So far we've performed more than 3000 concerts in 20 countries including 12 tours of Europe, more than 30 times across the United States and Canada, plus several trips into Mexico and Paraguay.

Not long after Christine and I were married, something very exciting happened. My phone rang and a deep voice asked: "Eduard Klassen?" "Yes," I replied.

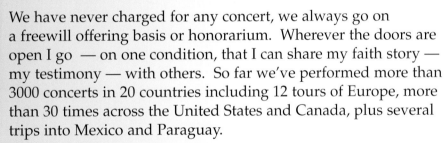

"I'm Craig Cook, Canadian Director of *Missionary Radio HCJB, (World Radio Missionary Fellowship)*. Someone told me about you and how, while you were in the jungles of Paraguay, you listened to our radio station *HCJB,* broadcasting from Quito, Ecuador, and how it has changed your life. I'd like to meet you."

*Wilfried, Viktor, Harold, Gustav, Eduard, Ronald*

Wow – this was amazing! I was actually going to meet in person someone whose voice I might have heard coming out of that little black box all those years ago. *'Hoy Christo Jesus Bendice"* are the call

*A*SOULFUL JOURNEY

letters in Spanish, translated, *"Today Christ Jesus Blesses!"* (Or in English, *Heralding Christ Jesus Blessings.)* It certainly had blessed me.

My First Recording 1985 in Paraguay

It was so wonderful to talk to Craig and others in the *HCJB* office and to learn more about how God in such amazing ways is blessing His gospel that goes out to people all around the world, from that mountain station in Ecuador. Truly, our God is an awesome God, I just couldn't stop marveling at how wonderful it all was.

It wasn't long before I also met the staff of *TWR, Trans World Radio* and learned about their amazing outreach to all parts of the globe. Both missions asked me to participate in their annual Partners Banquets to share my story of how missionary radio had reached so deep into an unreachable South American jungle, and lit a fire in a young boy's heart, and created a passion for Christian music that would not go away. Sharing at these banquets has been a great joy for me; I feel deeply honored to be able to encourage the men and women who through the years have faithfully supported such an amazing ministry.

I developed different styles of playing the favorite hymns that seemed to please and reach different people and they were asking for recordings.

So we began making cassette tapes, then VHS/DVDs and CDs, 16 to date. One of the first ones was with Latin style music and rhythm called *"Latin American Favourites"*. Soon we came up with another recording *"Be Still and Know"*. When children came into our lives, we recorded *"Children's Praise"*. Not long after came *"Because He Lives"*. One was a Christmas recording, *"Christmas Melodies"*. It was and still is a very popular album with Christmas traditional hymns. As I traveled with my singing harp, I

learned how much people like these hymns and more and more I thanked God for giving me this gift. Soon, a new recording came *"Great Is Thy Faithfulness"*. Great popularity was *"Melodies of the Heart"*, as well as later, *"Concert Album - The Music"*. Since Spanish audiences welcomed my music also with great warmth, the album *"Gracia Admirable"* followed soon, which is sung in Spanish. After several concerts in Germany, pretty well the same was

required, and recording *"Meine Lebensgeschichte"* - which is my lifestory in German. Similar autobiography - a Testimony in English was *"Out of the Paraguayan Chaco"*. My VHS and DVD *"The Story Behind My Music"*, is a collection of stories and music from a concert.

We now have a studio in our Stratford home where we are able to record our own tracks, then it goes to a professional studio in Toronto to finish the recording. I have wonderful Christian musicians to play with me. The two latest albums, *"Country & Bluegrass"*, and *"Folk Melodies"* were made in Nashville, USA.

Selling these recordings is what keeps us on the road so we can do this ministry. On tour, Christine mans the booth and sells recordings at our concerts. In North America, we travel now in a 27-foot motor home. God has blessed us with two fine sons, Mathias and Sheldon who travel with us. Christine home-schools the boys when we're on the road, and when we're home in Stratford, Ontario they attend a fine Christian school.

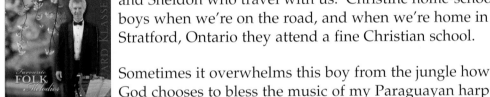

Sometimes it overwhelms this boy from the jungle how much God chooses to bless the music of my Paraguayan harp. So many people from around the world write to tell us they have been blessed and encouraged and have accepted Jesus Christ as Savior through the concerts. Others tell us they've come to the Lord just through listening to the music recordings.

Like the woman who came up to Christine after the concert to buy a CD. This was August just last summer, in Ontario, Canada. She chose a CD and told Christine, "This CD made my sister a Christian." Then she told Christine that her sister had been in hospital at death's door, she was full of cancer. But she was so angry at God she wouldn't let anyone talk about Him. One day this Christian lady took in one of my CDs and slipped it into her sister's player, and left it there. That night, as every night, the pain was so bad she couldn't sleep. In desperation she clicked on the CD player and the gentle music of those old hymns soothed her so that she fell asleep. For three days she listened to the music and when the sister came in she could tell her: "I've put my trust in Jesus, I know I'm ready for heaven." She died two days later.

I pray very much for God to guide me in what I should say when I go on stage. Because I don't want the people just to hear pretty music, my desire is that the music will speak to their hearts, and open them to hear God's voice. I want to say only what will help make this happen.

Usually I know what it will be, but sometimes when I get on stage, something totally different comes out. And so often I learn later that God had given me a special word to say to someone in the audience. That happened not long ago when I was playing in a little church north of Edmonton. Only a very few people were there. Afterwards, a dark-skinned lady came up and told me: "One sentence you said really touched my heart. I am a Muslim and after what you said tonight I want to give my life to Jesus Christ and know the freedom from slavery to sin that you talked about." Then she told me her husband had left just two days earlier.

'I'm at the end of my rope," she cried. The pastor led this dear broken woman to the Lord. She came into that little church a fearful, desperate Muslim, but she left a true Christian.

But first she was broken. And you know, dear brothers and sisters, that is when God will move in and work –when we're broken. When I broke in pieces before God, that is when God moved in and filled my life with joy and peace, and put me back together again – a clean, whole person, with nothing to hide.

God has filled my life with this wonderful joy. Only God can do that; the 'hype' of a big performance can't produce that kind of joy. It's there in the dark times and in the stormy, lonely times. People see that joy. And often they say it's that joy that draws them to want the Lord in their life. Sure, there are times when the going is rough. There are times when Satan tempts me to my old ways. But now I can say: "Satan, you lost that battle long ago, so get out of here."

It's so wonderful to be walking with God every day, walking and talking and praying all the time, night and day – there's never a time when I'm not in touch with my Lord. Sometimes we walk through a nice garden where everything is quiet and lovely, with no problems. But sometimes it's on a mountain top with the storm clouds and snow swirling around. Or in a wild valley where lions are waiting to pounce on me or my dear family.

But I've learned I can totally trust Him, at all times, and for all things. I know my God is not only with me, but by His Holy Spirit, He's in me.

And He goes ahead of me preparing the way, and preparing hearts for the message my harp will hopefully bring.
Whether the gathering is big or small, I'm always thankful for the opportunity to play beautiful music, and witness for my wonderful Lord.

I always have hope in the Lord, not just a hope of heaven when I die, but hope for blessings down here. Because God has promised *"Strength for today and bright hope for tomorrow – GREAT IS THY FAITHFULNESS"* — that's the song my harp often sings.

I thank God every day that He chose me and my family – my wife Christine and our two boys, and that we can travel all over the world and proclaim what Jesus has done for us.

Again and again I have thanked God for using me in a mighty way to praise His Name. I thank Him for the humble beginnings in a mud-brick house in Paraguay, for taking me to the city where I could study, and then make it to Europe, to Canada, and the USA.

And God wants to use all of us. Each single born-again Christian has a wonderful gift from God. I want to tell you that it's not about a diploma or a professional title we might have, it's about knowing Jesus Christ as our Lord and Savior. If we will love Him and serve Him from the bottom of our hearts, God will do awesome things through us. If we ask the Holy Spirit to guide us, He will do it, my friend. I might not be the most studied guy in the world, but I do love my Savior from the bottom of my heart. I want to use the time that I have left on this earth to glorify His name and encourage other Christians to walk with the Lord. I thank the Lord for all the amazing blessings that He has given me through these years.

For being able to share my story with a smile on my face,
with joy and hope,
and with a song in my heart.

*The Klassens in Canada 2005*

*"To God be the glory,
great things He has done!"*

**Eduard Klassen, May 2006**

*Our children Am Konigsee, Germany*
*Our children's first fish that they caught in Canada*
*Klassen Family Photo 2001*

About the Author

Eduard Klassen was born and raised in Paraguay, South America. Playing the harp has been his passion since 1975. Later in his life he studied music for 5 years in Asuncion. His tours have taken him to 20 countries where he has performed over 3,000 concerts. He has been in churches, schools, colleges, concert halls and on radio and television programs.

Eduard brought his musical skills and talent to Canada, where he presently resides in Ontario, with wife Christine and sons Mathias and Sheldon.

Christine Klassen was born and raised in Ontario, Canada, and has played the piano since 1976. She graduated as an R.N. in 1990. Currently Christine does not perform in concert with her husband Eduard.

*"I'm working for the Lord", says Eduard, "wherever He leads. In my life and in my travels I seek to uplift the Lord's name. I love to tell others what God has done for me. My desire is to use my gift of music and testimony to exhort and encourage other people in all walks of life. We appreciate your prayers and encouragement as we minister and travel in different countries. Thank you for supporting us in this way."*

The Paraguayan harp is a traditional folk instrument. Missionaries from Spain came in the 17th and 18th century with a classical harp. Natives, intrigued with the instrument, made some changes and claimed it as part of their culture.

The Paraguayan harp is made with a diatonic scale, with no foot pedals. It has only five octaves so the playing is somewhat limiting.
It is made of thin cedar and pine wood; thus it is lighter in weight than the classical harp. Because of the design, the sound is produced in two areas: by the vibration of the chords and from the vibration of the wide instrument. The harp is known in most South American countries, with each country adapting its own design, style and rhythms.